YOU AUTO SEE MAINE

Happy Motoring,

Will Anderson

To Catherine:
Thanks a Bunch, Honeybunch

When Old Cars Were Young And For Sale In Maine

YOU AUTO SEE MAINE

by Will Anderson

Anderson & Sons' Publishing Co.
34 Park Street
Bath, Maine 04530

Other Books By The Author

The Beer Book (1973)
The Beer Poster Book (1977)
Beer, New England (1988)
New England Roadside Delights (1989)
Mid-Atlantic Roadside Delights (1991)
Was Baseball Really Invented In Maine? (1992)
Good Old Maine (1993)
More Good Old Maine (1995)
The Great State Of Maine Beer Book (1996)
Where Have You Gone, Starlight Cafe? (1998)

Library of Congress Catalogue Card Number 99-72411

Will Anderson 1940 -
1. Popular Culture 2. Automobile/Transportation 3. Maine/New England

ISBN 1-893804-00-3

Studio Photography by A. & J. DuBois Commercial Photography, Lewiston, Maine
Typeset and printed by Spectrum Printing and Graphics, Auburn, Maine
Cover lamination by New England Finishing, Holyoke, Massachusetts
Bound by Bay State Bindery, Boston, Massachusetts
Text stock: 80lb. Somerset Gloss Recycled, S.D. Warren/Sappi North America, Skowhegan, Maine
Cover stock: 12pt. Kromekote, Champion International Corp., Hamilton, Ohio

Cover graphic: circa 1946 postcard view,
C.C. Banks & Son, Liberty, Maine. Courtesy of Blanche B. Martin, Bangor, Maine

Table of Contents

Acknowledgments

Many, many people were thoughtful enough to provide assistance in the researching of YOU AUTO SEE MAINE. I'd like to especially thank:

For their help with information research:

Karl Aromaa, Rumford Public Library, Rumford • Kathie Barrie, Portland Public Library, Portland • Prudence Barry, Portland Public Library, Portland • Wendy Lombard Bossie, Caribou Public Library, Caribou • Madeline Boudreau, Waterville Public Library, Waterville • Tom Brown, Maine Auto Dealers' Association, Augusta • Joyce Butler, Kennebunk • Ann Cough, Maine State Library, Augusta • Philip Crosby, Jr., Belfast • Paul D'Aessandro, Portland Public Library, Portland • Tom Gaffney, Portland Public Library, Portland • Carol Feurtado, Dexter Historical Society, Dexter • Joe Gill, Madison Public Library, Madison • Marilyn Hinkley, Yarmouth Historical Society, Yarmouth • Grant A. Jones, Ripley & Fletcher Co., South Paris •Denise Larson, Patton Free Library, Bath • Barbara McIntosh, *Lewiston Sun Journal*, Lewiston • Myrtle McKenna, Rumford Historical Society, Rumford • Julie R. Mowatt, Town of Bridgton, Bridgton • Peggy Newman, Ardmore Public Library, Ardmore, Pennsylvania • Ann Ridge, Portland Public Library, Portland • Randy Roberts, Thomaston • Sarah Sabasteanski, Auburn Public Library, Auburn • Anne Sheble, Waterville Public Library, Waterville • Lyn Sudlow, Falmouth Public Library, Falmouth • Pauline Wyman, Farmington Public Library, Farmington

For their help with photo research:

Peter D. Bachelder, Ellsworth • Mara Buck, Windsor • Bob Filgate, McArthur Public Library, Biddeford • Faith Francis, Forest City Chevrolet/Saab, Portland • Julliete Gallant, Lewiston • Phil Gemmer, Forest City Chevrolet/Saab, Portland • Dayton Grandmaison, Van Buren •Tom Hug, Lorain, Ohio • Ruth Kane, Ellsworth • Micheal Lord, Androscoggin Historical Society, Auburn • Blanche B. Martin, Bangor • Peter A. Moore, York • Mike Murphy, Katahdin Motors, Millinocket • Trudy Price, Woolwich • Stephanie Philbrick, Maine Historical Society, Portland • Barbara D. Poulin, South China • Earle Shuttleworth, Maine Historic Preservation Commission, Augusta • Vic J. Thompson, Houlton • Todd Wenzel, Forest City Chevrolet/Saab, Portland • Gale Yohe, Hollis

Circa 1915 "comic" postcard

Introduction

I grew up in the 1940s/1950s when you could tell one car from another. A Ford looked different than a Packard. A Buick looked different than a DeSoto. And a Studebaker looked different than them all. Were those years the "Golden Years?" I don't know. When it comes to cars there have been a lot of "Golden Years." YOU AUTO SEE MAINE pays tribute to most of them.

The book is divided into four parts. Part I features 63 past and present (mostly past) Maine auto dealers and some of the cars they sold. They are presented in dealer-ad chronological order. The 63 *are not* meant to highlight the biggest or the longest lasting dealers. Or those that are/were the best known. They are meant to be representative of large and small. Of shortlived and longlived. Of the entire state. From York County to The County. They are also meant to showcase ads that I consider attractive or intriguing. The auto write-ups, on the other hand, *are* meant to include the best-known makes, but there is a rich dose of long gone/long forgotten names, too. (When, for example, was the last time you really gave any honest thought to a Winton or a Whippet?).

Part II, which interweaves with Part I, is entitled Motoring Along and is designed to give a decade-by-decade overview of auto happenings. I began with the noble intention of reading six decades of yesteryear's Portland, Bangor, Lewiston, perhaps even Augusta, newspapers. I soon realized, however, that I'd be reading forever. The result, since I lived in the "Forest City" at the time, was to bail out and go with basically just Portland, primarily the *Sunday Telegram*. The cuts used to illustrate Part II are from the *Telegram* , too. I did, though, work hard to find facts and fancy from all over, not only Portland. And the jokes, corny but very period, are certainly representative of the entire state.

7

The news clips selected are meant to give a feeling for those early days when cars were truly "horseless carriages," when to speed was to "scorch," to flip over to "turn turtle." To those not-so-early days when FDR urged a top speed of 40 miles per hour "for the duration," Crosley was introduced as the ultimate economy car, and Buick featured Dynaflow Drive. To those relatively recent days when, in a nationwide poll, women reported they'd rather be stranded on a desert island with a car salesman than anyone else, Sears unveiled its own auto (the Allstate), and actress Piper Laurie declared that women were better drivers than men.

Both Parts I and II come to a screeching halt in 1959 because, in my view at least, after that boredom and sameness arrived on the American auto scene to stay. There was also the matter of book size. Had I continued on for another decade or more it would have necessitated adding 20 or 30 more pages. It would have been too much.

Part III points up some of the remnants that yet survive from Maine's colorful automobile past. The four pages included are but the tip of an iceberg of consequence. Poke around: there's a lot more out there both in the way of showrooms and "auto rows," and fading "ghost" signs. How much good stuff can you find?

MOTORING IN MAINE HAS ITS DRAWBACKS

People early-on figured out that Maine had its own special obstacles when it came to happy motoring. This is a reproduction from the January 7, 1909 issue of the original LIFE magazine.

A. C. MAXIM

DEALER IN

𝕱lour and 𝕱eed of 𝕬ll 𝕶inds

AT WHOLESALE AND RETAIL

All the leading poultry supplies on hand

Agent For **Reo Motor Cars**

WE SELL
Gasolene, Ever Ready Flashlights,
AUTOMOBILE SUPPLIES,
Books, Everything Electrical, and
Oakland Automobiles,
"STURDY AS THE OAK"
NEWLANDS COMPANY,
MERRIMAN BUILDING,
Telephone 117-12 LIVERMORE FALLS

Well into the pre-Great War years there were those who hedged their bets with respect to selling cars. The A.C. Maxim/Reo ad (from South Paris) dates from 1912; the Newlands/Oakland ad from 1916.

Last comes Part IV, a capsule look at the Pine Tree State's noteworthy still-in-operation diners, drive-in theatres, auto museums, and antique auto shows. They're all well worth supporting.

A PAIR OF ADDITIONAL NOTES

It should be noted that, while YOU AUTO SEE MAINE includes a solid representation of the many, many auto makes and models that have been *sold* in Maine down through the years, it does not delve into those autos *manufactured* in Maine. For input on that subject look for the very thorough A HISTORY OF MAINE BUILT AUTOMOBILES by Richard and Nancy Fraser of East Poland. For further information on each and every auto ever produced in America, THE STANDARD CATALOG OF AMERICAN CARS, compiled and edited by Beverly Rae Kimes and Henry Austin Clark, Jr., is invaluable. I relied on it considerably for the auto write-ups included in Part I.

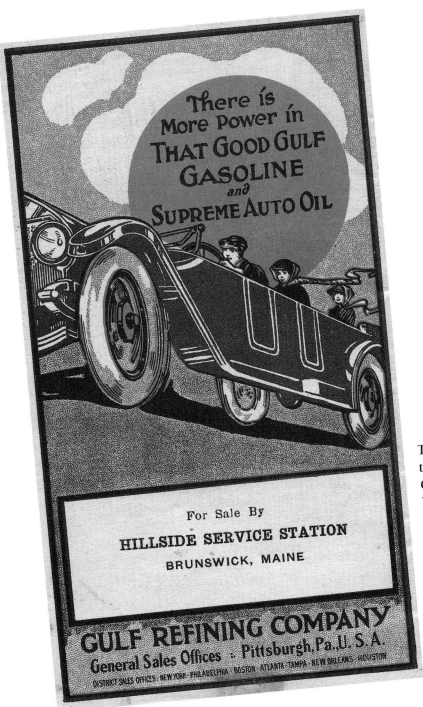

This is the back cover of a nifty little booklet, entitled The Motorists' Convenient Record of Lubrication, Tires and Gasoline, that was handed out by Gulf in the 1920s. The Hillside Service Station, owned by one Alonzo Tyler, operated on the Bath Road in Brunswick for a short period in the early 1920s.

World War II You
Auto Be My
Valentine card

AND LAST

The ads used to illustrate YOU AUTO SEE MAINE are from period automobile and mass circulation magazines, newspapers, souvenir programs, school publications, etc. While the bulk of the material is from my own collection, I am very thankful to quite a number of other people and organizations that graciously lent me photographs, postcards and the like. These good people/organizations are included in both the Acknowledgments and via the "Courtesy of..." legend beside each such applicable graphic.

The information included in the history of the 63 auto dealers that are included in Part 1 came by way of town and city directories, newspapers of the day, death records, and personal accounts where possible. By last count I had researched - in person - in 18 local public libraries, from Kennebunk and Biddeford to Caribou and Houlton, from Rumford and Madison to Bath and Damariscotta. Plus the Maine and Pejepscot Historical Societies and the Maine State Library. And, by mail and phone, with others, most notably the Dexter and Rumford Historical Societies.

Thank you one and all.

You auto see Maine.

Motoring Along:

1908

1900

A Good Roads discussion in Portland was attended by a large gathering of horsemen and bicyclists. At least one automobilist showed up, and spoke out. Said the automobilist, a Mr. C.H. Simonds: "If I should drive through one of the Portland streets as fast as I did in Massachusetts I would expect to land in Biddeford in a heap." (February)

Charles W. Morse (as in Morse High School) brought an auto from New York to Maine to give to his two sons who lived in Bath. "It is," wrote *The Bangor Daily News*, "the first horseless carriage to be owned in Bath and is attracting much attention." (May)

In an article on Bangor's first automobile, the BDN had some fun and penned "The auto has come to Bangor...and all the horses are switching their tails in envy." Continued the paper's scribe: "Auto, you know, is short for automobile, just like photo for photograph, and so on." (May)

The Lewiston Evening Journal noted "Four automobiles in Bar Harbor and more coming." (June)

Statistics compiled by the city assessor's office showed Bangor with 1963 horses, 586 bicycles, one automobile. (June)

Francis E. Stanley (of Stanley brothers' fame) made what was headlined "A NEW RECORD" when he drove his auto from Newton, Mass. to Portland in six hours and ten minutes. "The prodigious part of this road record for automobilism," stressed the *Lewiston Evening Journal*, lay in the fact that Mr. Stanley was carrying three passengers plus himself and had, as well, to put up with "very defective" roads for much of the way between Portsmouth and Portland. (June)

The Portland *Evening Express* observed, in its Yarmouth notes, that "Mr. Meldon H. Merrill will be the most popular young man in town for the next two weeks. He has just returned from Boston, bringing an elegant automobile. Being of a generous disposition he will undoubtedly give all his friends the novel experience of a ride in a horseless carriage." (August)

1901

In what may be Maine's first gasoline sales pitch, N.D. Winslow, 90 Preble Street, Portland, advertised "Fill Your Automobile With Winslow's Gasoline." Continued the ad, in the *Evening Express* of April 6th, "Best quality. Prices right." and, believe it or not, "Let me call on you." (April)

Auto owners held a meeting at M.D. Hanson's studio in Portland to discuss the formation of an automobile club in Maine. "It is hoped," noted the *Evening Express*, "to include in the membership every owner of an automobile in the state." (Ed. note: Maynard D. Hanson, a photographer with a studio at Monument Square, is credited with being the first person in Portland to own an auto. It was a Stanley, and it arrived by boat from Boston on July 19, 1899.). (April)

In what may be Maine's first used car ad, H.M. Jones, 33 Pearl Street, Portland, ran an announcement in the *Lewiston Evening Journal* that read: "FOR SALE. My last year's Locomobile. Run less than 1500 miles. In good condition. Price $600.00." (May)

1900-1909

It was reported in the *Evening Express* that Charles Dunn was utilizing a "horseless wagon" on his milk route, the first milkman in Portland to do so. (June)

The LEJ noted, in its Up in Maine column, that "Canaan saw its first automobile last week and again we realize that the world does move." (July)

The Portland *Sunday Telegram* ran a front-page article, headlined "Automobiles Are Now Common In Portland," and then proceeded to list the name and occupation of each and every car owner in the city and surrounding area. (Ed. note: there were 30 in all, with the great majority being Stanleys.) (July)

Big news in Westbrook: the *Evening Express* reported that "Saturday afternoon an automobile, managed by a lady, attracted much attention on Main street. The lady occupant was Mrs. Alice Sisson of Front street. Mrs. Sisson appeared fully capable of handling the machine, and successfully accomplished the journey to the neighboring town of Gorham and return without a mishap. It was," closed the *Express*, "her second attempt at handling an automobile." (July)

Wrote the *Lewiston Evening Journal*: "Lubec is decidedly up-to-date; it has a horseless patrol wagon in its police department." (September)

1902

Mr. and Mrs. George Sawyer of Portland, upon returning from a trip to Massachusetts in their brand new White Steamer, proclaimed that "This carriage is a dream and riding in it seems like riding in a parlor car on a railroad train." (June)

Beaconstreet: "Did your ancestors come over on the Mayflower?"

Struckoil: "Certainly not. They came in an automobile."

Evening Express (July)

In its "Automobile Bubbles" column, the LEJ spelled

out what an automobilist should do upon meeting a horse: Stop the vehicle and, if the horse is frightened, turn off the engine. "If there is any difficulty the driver of the automobile should lead the horse himself or have him led past the vehicle. In doing this the man leading the horse should pass between the animal and the motor (car), as it will partially conceal it from his (the animal's) sight. The occupant of the auto should also call out to the horse and say 'Whoa' in a loud voice, which will often reassure the animal." (July)

Knicker: Leroy says he must cut down expenses. Can't afford to support a wife and five children and keep an automobile going any longer."

Bocker: "Can't he get some of his friends to adopt the children?"

Evening Express (November)

1903

At a meeting of the Brewer City Council, a Mr. Elmer Goss took the floor. He stated that at a recent Grange meeting a topic for discussion was Good Roads, "but after they had got at the topic they found that there were no good roads to discuss and so they changed the subject to Bad Roads." (May)

The 4th of July parade in the Perryville section of Auburn featured what was described by the LEJ as "whole squadrons of autos in rank and file." Represented was the Rambler, the Oldsmobile, and a host of Stanley Steamers.

The LEJ "Among The Automobilists" columnist waxed that "The sport of automobiling is at its summer high tide of interest in these cities... there is a veritable automobile fever... and the fever is spreading in various new directions." (July)

Two men made the first San Francisco-to-Portland transcontinental "run," arriving in Portland on September 23rd, 48 days and 5,100 miles after they'd set out. Their vehicle: an Oldsmobile that weighed in at 800 pounds!

The story goes that a Saco skunk was making his way along the road when he saw an auto making its way toward him. Mr. Skunk had never before seen an auto, so he looked wonderingly at the oncoming monster and decided to salute it in his characteristic manner. The horseless car flew by with a smell of smoke, gasolene and oil. Mr. Skunk looked in amazement, threw his head into the air, sniffed and with a disgusted expression, exclaimed: "Oh, Lord, what's the use!"

Portland Daily Advertiser (December)

1904

"Young Faddlethwaite doesn't seem to have any moral courage," said her father.

"I don't know about that," she answered, "but he has splendid fitting clothes and three automobiles."

Portland Evening Express (January)

The LEJ reported that there were over 300 owners of automobiles in Maine, with 83 of them residing in Portland. (May)

Mr. Ernest C. Cox, of Boston, visiting Portland and Bangor with his wife in their gasoline touring car, was quoted as saying that Maine exceeded all other states in "fine scenery, steep hills and bad roads." (June)

A couple from New Jersey, Mr. and Mrs. Elliot Johnson of South Orange, took an early autumn trip to northern Maine where, per an account in *The Portland Daily Advertiser*, "they passed through territory never before visited by automobilists." The result wasn't good: the area natives "were in mortal fear of the machine." At first the Johnsons "enjoyed the sensation they made but when the residents refused to shelter either the automobile or the tourists it ceased," they said, "to be a joke." (September)

Lewiston automotive pioneer J.W. Skene advertised "Anyone buying a Phonograph at my place will receive an Automobile Ride FREE to their home together with the Phonograph, if desired." (December)

1905

The *Washington Post* presented two very different views of motoring. Rudyard Kipling was quoted as saying that "The development of the motor car has benefited mankind, spiritually, physically, and mentally," while S. Lewes Dickinson, characterized as "an English author of some repute," was said to have stated that "automobiling is a stated pernicious manifestation of the almost universal desire to rush and hurry and is detrimental to calm and steady mental progress." (May)

1906

It was announced that 85,000 automobiles were in use in the U.S. at the end of 1905. Maine was calculated to have 731 of them. And in the *Sunday Telegram*, issue of February 25, all 731 were listed, starting with registrant number one (R.H. Ingersoll of Biddeford, who owned a Rambler) and proceeding right down to number 731 (Orrel A. Gooch of East Machias, who owned a Locomobile). (February)

Among a list of "Rules For An Automobile" found in the *Telegram* were the following, obviously written by someone with a sense of humor: "If your carburetor doesn't work, taste the gasoline and sweeten until right;" "To repair a bad tire, use about equal parts of tire tape and profanity;" and, my favorite, "Should your hill climber give out do not get rattled. Alight with easy grace from the machine, and then allow it to roll backwards down the hill." (February)

H.J. Willard Co., Portland, in an ad headlined "Winton Automobiles Are Doing Well," announced that a Winton Model K had made a run to "Two Lights and Back with Nine People in 67 Minutes. It was not a wonderful feat," the ad continued, "but it shows what a Winton will do on roads around home." (June)

Buick began what became the norm when it introduced its next year's model the previous fall; i.e., its 1907 models in 1906. As Buick ads read: "If you want a car for next season, why not have the use of it this Fall?" (September)

A trio from Windham, Arthur Smith, William Taylor, and Harry McNally, took an auto trip to Boston and had so many mishaps (including getting stuck in deep mud, and then having a run-in with a horse and buggy, both in Saco) that they left their car - to be picked up at "a later and more convenient date" - in the Hub and took the train home. (November)

1907

The *Portland Sunday Telegram* ran an article headlined "AUTO FAD IS NOT DYING OUT," in which they made it clear that those who thought the auto would follow the fate of the bicycle were wrong." (January)

Maine's speed limits were 8/15: eight miles an hour in cities, towns and built-up areas; 15 miles an hour elsewhere. Regardless of location, speed had to always be "reasonable." (February)

Goding's Boot and Shoe Store, Rumford, advertised the "Queen Quality" Auto Boot as a fine Christmas gift. "It is very stylish," promised the ad. (December)

1908

The *Sunday Telegram* heralded the fact that mssrs. James A. Marr and Fred Togue made the trip from Portland to Bangor in five hours and 45 minutes… considered quite the feat given the time of year and that between Pittsfield and Bangor the duo made the run in heavy rain. "The car (an Oldsmobile roadster) and the drivers were hardly recognizable, so covered with mud were they, and their arrival in Bangor created quite a sensation." (January)

Portland's George E. Huff began the manufacture of portable automobile houses (garages). "The house," it was said, "is constructed of galvanized iron and is easily and quickly put together." (April)

The Portsmouth-Portland road was reported to be in especially bad shape, with the stretch through Thornton Heights in South Portland the worst. Sand there was almost hub deep, with the result that unknowing drivers were almost certain to incur serious damage to their autos. (June)

Mrs. George E. Riggs (far better known as Kate Douglas Wiggin) of Hollis purchased a Reo touring car. (August)

1909

Mr. E.C. McDonald, general manager of the Graphophone Co. of Bridgeport, Connecticut, toured Maine in a Pierce-Arrow. Said Mr. McDonald: "A beautiful, beautiful state, magnificent scenery, but oh dear, what roads." (August)

The Harmon Automobile Co., Portland, advertised the rental of "finely equipped, up-to-date cars by the day or hour. This is," noted the ad, "a very pleasant way to entertain your out of town friends." (December)

1909

The Taxicab Company of Maine inaugurated taxi service in Portland. (March)

A royal blue Pierce-Arrow enclosed auto was ordered for the use of president-elect William Taft and his family. (Ed. note: "Big Bill" needed a big car; he tipped the scales at a hefty 325 pounds when he took office!) (February)

"Auto Fever Hits Gardiner, Maine" headlined a special to the *Telegram*, making it be known that the number of autos in Gardiner had jumped by 50% from last summer. "Gardiner has been slow in getting the automobile fever, but it has got it," closed out the story. (May)

Helen Lawrence of Saco was honored as the youngest licensed driver in Maine. Then 13, Miss Lawrence had been licensed for two years, and was said to be happiest when at the wheel of her family's runabout.

F.O. BAILEY
PORTLAND

James Monroe was in the White House and the War of 1812 was a recent memory. It was 1819... the year Henry Bailey launched what became F.O. Bailey. "F.O." stood for Frederick O., and he was Henry's son. He took over, in 1867, a business that has traditionally been auctioneering. Traditionally, but not always. Through the decades the F.O. Bailey company has been involved in many ventures. Pioneer automobile sales was one. As early as 1901 the F.O. Bailey Carriage Company (a subsidiary of F.O. Bailey, located at 163-165 Middle Street, that made and sold carriages, sleighs, horse/stable equipment, etc.) advertised itself as "State agents for Locomobiles." (Ed. note: the Locomobile was a much respected car manufactured in Bridgeport Conn., from 1900 to 1929.). Within little more than a year White, Winton, Stanley, and the Waverly were added to the mix. The result was a need for more space; accomplished by a move to the brand new "Automobile Station," at 44 Plum Street, heralded here. There followed Peerless, Stevens-Duryea, and Rambler. By 1905, however, the company had spun the bulk of its auto sales off to another subsidiary, the Maine Motor Carriage Co. (q.v.). The F.O. Bailey Carriage Company kept its hand in the auto business, though, representing such as Pullman ("The best in the $800 class ever offered in this State") and Velie ("The design of this car is extremely artistic and original"). It also sold the line of both Brockway and Republic trucks at their 163-165 Middle Street location.

It's now 1999. Bill Clinton is in the White House and the War of 1812 isn't a hot topic anymore. The F.O. Bailey Carriage Company is long gone. But F.O. Bailey, now located at 141 Middle, is still going strong. Some things don't change. (Ed. note: Plum Street, site of F.O. Bailey's historic "Automobile Station," ran from Fore to Middle streets, roughly halfway between Exchange and Union. It is a street that no longer exists.).

AUTOMOBILE
Exhibition and Opening.

The week commencing Monday, the 31st, we shall hold an exhibition of Automobiles to inaugurate the opening of our new Automobile Station, No. 44 Plum street, near Middle. At a great deal of cost and painstaking, we have combined the successful automobiles of America under one roof, as follows:

STEAM MACHINES.

The **WHITE** automobile, the wonder and winner of records in the Endurance Test last fall. Price $1200.

The **LOCOMOBILE,** old and reliable favorite, $850 to $2500.

The **STANLEY,** result of years of experience combined with economy. Price $600.

GAS MACHINES.

The **WINTON,** the oldest and most experienced manufacturers in America of Hydro-carbon vehicles. Price $1200.

ELECTRIC MACHINES.

The **WAVERLY,** undoubtedly the best. Price $800.

Experienced demonstrators will assist our own during the week. We would be pleased to give anyone a ride who is interested.

Open all the week until 10 p. m.

F. O. BAILEY CARRIAGE CO.,

Opposite Post Office.

Ad, *Portland Daily Advertiser,* April 1, 1902

THIS picture shows Pope Waverley Surrey, Price $1,500. This carriage combines more utility, convenience and style than any other automobile for general family use.

ELECTRICS

Are always ready, clean, noiseless, and so simple any member of the family can operate them.

Our 1904 Catalogue shows runabouts, stanhopes, chelseas, station, physicians and delivery wagons. Agents in principal cities.

POPE MOTOR CAR CO., Waverley Department, **Indianapolis, Ind.**

WAVERLY/POPE-WAVERLY

The Waverly Electric was successfully produced in Indianapolis from 1898 to 1903. In fact, General Lew Wallace, the author of BEN HUR, was known to have purchased a Waverly surrey in 1902. The car's name was changed in 1904 to the Pope-Waverly (representative of the fact that it was part of the empire of early auto magnate Albert Augustus Pope) and it was produced, increasingly less successfully, until 1908, when Pope management ceased operations in Indianapolis. New interests then stepped in, however, dropped the "Pope," and continued to produce Waverlys until 1916. In that year production ceased for good.

THE JAMES BAILEY COMPANY
PORTLAND

The James Bailey Company is well remembered. It should be: it was around a long time, beginning in 1846 with the sale of saddle and hardware goods. Autos were added right after the turn of the century, most likely in 1901. Mr. Bailey chose well, too, selecting the Oldsmobile. Other makes that James Bailey represented were the Toledo Steam Carriage and the Stanley. But auto supplies and apparel were more to James Bailey's liking than the autos themselves, and by 1906 the James Bailey Company had sold its last automobile. Bicycle sales and service, tire repair, and the sale of sports apparel and equipment (as well as auto supplies and specialties): these were the James Bailey Company's bread and butter, spread over the company's two locations, 18 Free Street and 264 Middle Street. For a time, in and around 1913, the James Bailey Company served as local agent for Harley Davidson.

In 1941, just five years short of its 100th birthday, the James Bailey Company passed out of Bailey family control. In 1986 operations were moved from 264 Middle Street in downtown Portland to the "greener pastures" of the Maine Mall area. In 1987 the company went out of business.

A Speed of 15 3.4 miles per hour, maintained for eight hours in a run from Boston to Portland, was the record made by the

OLDSMOBILE

on Sunday last. The carriage contained two passengers and came through without delay or difficulty of any kind. East of Portsmouth the roads were especially bad, but it was all the same to this sturdy little carriage. All told, over 126 miles were covered, one or two slight detours being made

THE JAMES BAILEY CO., AGTS.
18 Free Street.
tu th sat

Ad, *Portland Daily Advertiser,*
May 20, 1902

AN ANNOUNCEMENT.

We have established at No. 18 Free St. a department for the sale of Carriages and Automobiles and have arranged for the exclusive agency of a number of the leading carriage manufactories in the country.

We shall also have the local representation of the celebrated Olds-mobile Gasoline Automobile and the Toledo Steam Carriage, each of which respectively is of the highest representative type of gasoline and steam propelled vehicles.

We extend a cordial invitation to old customers and new to visit us at our Free street store, and we assure them of the same policy of fair treatment in this new branch of our business as has characterized our trade dealings for upwards of half a century.

Very respectfully,
The JAMES BAILEY COMPANY,
264 Middle Street.   18 Free Street.

Ad, *Portland Daily Advertiser,*
April 3, 1902

Ad, *Motor* magazine, April 1918

STANLEY

Volumes could and have been written on the Stanley twins, Francis E. ("Frank") and Freelan O. ("Freel"). Born June 1, 1849 in Kingfield, the brothers lived the first forty years of their lives in Maine, where they established the highly successful Stanley Dry Plate Co. In 1889 the twins moved operations to greater Boston. By the late 1890s they were "into" horseless carriages and the very limited production of light steam-powered vehicles. And by 1899 it was full-steam (Ed. note: sorry, I couldn't resist) ahead with automobiles.

Renowned for their speed and their hill-climbing ability, Stanleys were produced until 1924. Peak production was 1907, when 775 units came rolling out of the brothers' Newton, Massachusetts factory. By 1924 that figure was down to 102. Francis died in 1918; Freelan in 1940. There is today a museum in Kingfield, the Stanley Museum, in the brothers' honor.

H.J. WILLARD
PORTLAND

Portland automotive pioneer number three was a man named H. (for Herbert) J. Willard. As early as 1903 Willard ran an ad in THE MAINE REGISTER (sort of an early state-wide Yellow Pages) billing himself as an agent for "Reliable and Satisfactory Automobiles." And The Portland Sunday Telegram, in a February 1906 article, termed Willard and his firm "perhaps one of the greatest factors in automobiledom in the State of Maine...showing the very best there is in the newest models of up to date automobiles." Willard also had, for the time, quite an up-to-date line-up of models. At one time or other he was agent for Packard, Peerless, Pierce Stanhope, Franklin, Winton, Cadillac, Elmore, Buick, and, of course, Autocar. Willard's address changes were numerous as well. After starting out at 234 Middle Street, he made showroom moves to 18 Forest Avenue (where he named his endeavor the Congress Square Automobile Station and promised "Bargains in New and Second-Hand Machines"), 642 Congress Street (beneath the Lafayette Hotel), and, finally, 573 Congress. Also maintained was a service garage at 240-244 Spring Street.

All went seemingly well until 1907 when Willard, for reasons unknown, relocated to Providence, Rhode Island.

Photo, *Portland Sunday Telegram*, February 25, 1906

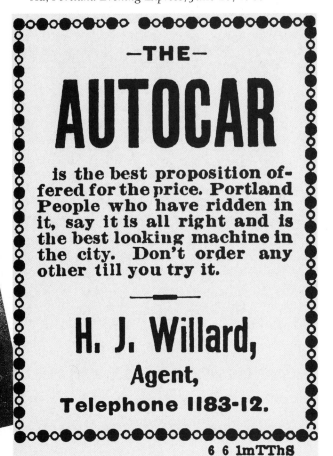

Type XV—$800.

The Autocar

The one motor car that has successfully taken the place of the horse in the physician's professional rounds. It is less expensive to maintain, easier to run and care for and is capable of unlimited work. So many physicians use The Autocar Runabout in their daily calls that it has become generally known as **The Doctor's Car**

The car comes to you fully equipped with top, storm apron, gas lamps, gas generator, horn, etc. 12 horse-power, three speeds and reverse, direct shaft drive. Autocar patented control—spark and throttle governed by grips in rim of steering wheel—a valuable advantage. Write for catalogue.

The Autocar Co.   **Ardmore, Pa.**

AUTOCAR

Today Autocar is best recalled - when it's recalled at all - as a manufacturer of trucks. That makes sense: the Autocar Company, located first in Ardmore and then in Exton, Pennsylvania (both just west of Philadelphia), manufactured high-grade commercial vehicles through the early 1980s. Autocar's roots, however, were more compatible with its name. Passenger cars were produced as early as 1901 and were continued through 1911. Peak production was 823 units in 1907.

RUSSELL AUTOMOBILE STATION LEWISTON

In 1904 longtime Auburn Fish Hatchery employee Ira F. Russell decided a career change was in order. He teamed up with an associate named Charles P. Butler to get in on the ground floor of the business of automobiles. It was to be a short-lived floor, though. Within three years Russell and Butler and their enterprise at 53 Middle Street were, for reasons unknown, a part of history. (Ed. note: Ira Russell is included in *YOU AUTO SEE MAINE* primarily because of his use of the term "Automobile Station," a name that was generally used for the earliest auto showrooms...but a name that, like Ira Russell, was destined to be around but a short time.).

JACKSON

The Jackson was one of several long-time-ago autos produced in Jackson, Michigan, a city about 65 miles due west of Detroit that undoubtedly had visions of motor car stardom for itself. It failed, as did the Jackson (which lasted from 1903 to 1923). (Ed. note: the Jackson's actual slogan, in those days of hill-climbing prowess, was the rather clever "No Hill Too Steep, No Sand Too Deep." Ira Russell had the right idea, but the wrong words.).

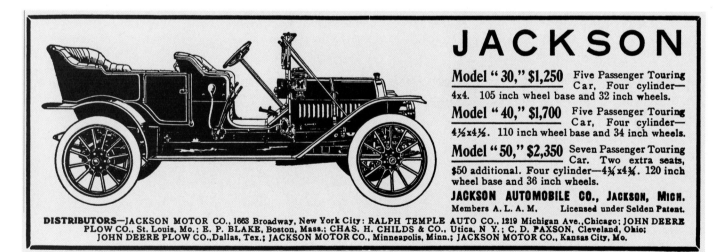

Ad, *The Horseless Age*, May 25 1910

23

L.C. GILSON AUTOMOBILE CO.
PORTLAND

L.C. Gilson was one of the many early auto dealers who preferred his initials to his name. His name was "Luther." Friends called him "Gill." Gilson's introduction to personal transportation came via the bicycle business in Portland in 1887. It was then on to the James Bailey Company (q.v.) and the auto. In late 1905 Gill went out on his own, constructing the state-of-the-art facility shown here. Located at 881-891 Congress Street, it was said to be the first structure in Maine built ground up as a garage. A write-up of the day extolled it in every way, proclaiming "it contains every comfort for patron and employee."

As was often the case during those early experimental days, Gilson was agent for an oft-changing array of autos. Included at one time or another was Maxwell, Ford, Reo, Premier, Stanley, Krit, Studebaker, Chevrolet, Briscoe, Columbia, and, longest running, the Mitchell ("The best Motor Car that $1,500 can buy").

In the spring of 1916 L.C. Gilson moved his company - now called the Gilson Auto Co. - closer to downtown, to 664 Congress Street, under the Lafayette Hotel. Later moves were to 315 Forest Avenue (1917-1920), and 355-357 Forest (1920-1924). The Gilson Auto Co. ceased operations in 1924. But motor sales were in L.C. Gilson's blood: he sold trucks for International Harvester until his death, from a heart attack, on April 13, 1931. Appropriately, he died while riding in his car.

Photo and sketch, *Portland Sunday Telegram*, February 25, 1906

NEW GARAGE OF L. C. GILSON AUTOMOBILE COMPANY.

24

MAXWELL

Named after an engineer named Jonathan D. Maxwell, the Maxwell was a well-respected make for two decades, 1905-1925. In and around 1910, in fact, it ranked third in sales, behind only Ford and Buick. Manufactured primarily in Tarrytown, New York, it was also produced in branch plants in New Castle, Indiana; Pawtucket and Cranston, Rhode Island; Auburn, New York; and Detroit.

The Maxwell was merged into the brand-new Chrysler Corporation in 1925. (Walter Chrysler was, in fact, Maxwell's last president.). Production ceased that same year.

THE MAXWELL WINS

The four cylinder MAXWELL, without any tuning up, and after having been driven from Tarrytown, N. Y., to Boston through the snow Friday and Saturday.

Won the Parker Hill Climbing Contest and $200 Cash Prize against a four cylinder Jackson, winning two straight heats.

THE MAXWELL
GENTLEMEN'S SPEEDISTER

Also climbed the hill with five persons aboard and without the use of chains. This is a wonderful performance considering that there were some four cylinder high powered cars that were stalled in their attempt to make the ascent

...Better Buy a Maxwell...

L. C. Gilson Automobile Co.
881 TO 891 CONGRESS STREET

Ad, *Portland Sunday Telegram*, March 25, 1906

MAINE MOTOR CARRIAGE COMPANY PORTLAND

The Maine Motor Carriage Company was an off-shoot of the F.O. Bailey Company (q.v.). By 1902 Bailey's automobile department at 163-165 Middle Street was about to burst. The solution was to start a new firm (Maine Motor Carriage) at a new location (85 Exchange Street). At the helm as manager was A.M. Spear, Jr., an experienced auto man who'd been with F.O. Bailey since 1899. Spear left in 1906 and was replaced by Brunswick native George A. Wagg, Jr. That same year the company also moved, engaging the respected architectural firm of John Calvin and John Howard Stevens to convert an almost 100-year old mansion into a noteworthy showroom and service center at 101 Free Street. Regardless of manager or address, though, one thing held constant: Maine Motor Carriage (changed to Maine Motor Car in 1912) liked variety. In its decade and a half of existence it was agent, at one time or another, for Oldsmobile, Stevens-Duryea (an August 1906 Maine Motor Carriage ad for Stevens-Duryea closed with "Ask the man who owns one," a slogan to be made considerably more famous by Packard), Haynes, Thomas, Pope-Tribune, Pope-Hartford, Peerless, E-M-F, Flanders, Saxon (lauded by Maine Motor Car as a "wonderful little car"), Chalmers, Paige-Detroit, National (touted as "A machine that will stand sledge hammer blows and still run regularly"), Jackson, and Marmon. Fourteen cars in fifteen years. That's variety.

A July 1, 1917 announcement in the *Portland Sunday Telegram* stated that the Maine Motor Company, with E.B. Brewer as president and treasurer, "succeeds the Maine Motor Car Company." No other information was given.

Ad, *Pine Tree Magazine*, June 1906

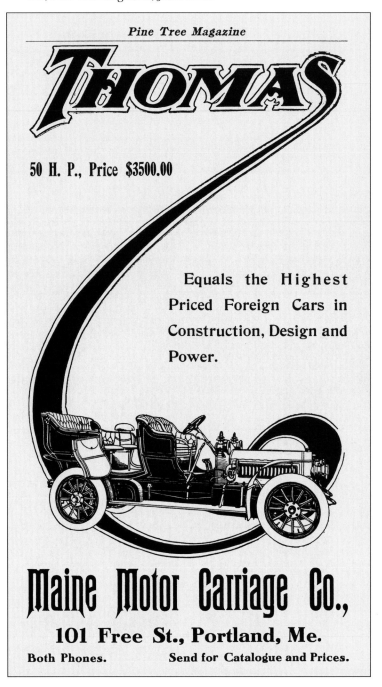

Pine Tree Magazine

THOMAS

50 H. P., Price $3500.00

Equals the Highest Priced Foreign Cars in Construction, Design and Power.

Maine Motor Carriage Co.,

101 Free St., Portland, Me.

Both Phones.   Send for Catalogue and Prices.

THE THOMAS
PHAETON

THE COMFORTABLE THOMAS

With its mechanical and structural features the efficiency of which is easily proven by demonstration, the 1912 Thomas marks an epoch in *automobile riding comfort*.

The eleven inch upholstering, the three quarter elliptic springs, the secondary springs, the shock absorbers and recoil straps give a degree of *tonneau comfort*, especially in touring, not yet attained by any other American or foreign car.

The underslung gasoline and oil tanks give an extremely low center of gravity causing the car to hold the road better at high speeds and on sharp turns and further enhance the *physical comfort* of the passengers.

The sturdy Thomas construction, the extra large brakes, the safety loops and the wonderfully strong yet easily controlled steering mechanism give ample assurance of safety and *mental comfort* to both driver and passengers.

FOUR STYLES OF OPEN BODIES —TOURING CAR, PHAETON, SURREY AND RUNABOUT, PRICE $4,000 FOR EACH TYPE.

Our Catalog —"The Story of the Thomas" awaits your request.

E. R. THOMAS MOTOR CAR COMPANY, DEPT. K. BUFFALO

THOMAS

E. (Erwin) R. Thomas turned from the manufacture of bicycles to the manufacture of autos in 1899, calling his machine the "Buffalo," after the city in New York in which it was made. In 1903 he decided a different name was in order. He chose "Thomas." During its early years the Thomas won considerable note as a racing car. During its latter years the company was perhaps best known for its taxicabs. Production ceased in 1918.

Ad, *Collier's* magazine, May 11, 1912

F. A. NICKERSON COMPANY
PORTLAND

F. (Fred) A. Nickerson was a Belfast native who made good - very good - in the automotive business in Portland. After having experimented, according to early articles, with self-propelled vehicles for better than two decades, "Nick" arrived in Portland in late 1906, setting up a showroom and sales office at 642 Congress, under the Lafayette Hotel. The automobile he sold: the Pierce-Arrow.

Nickerson was a success from the start. Oldsmobile was added in 1907 and received a nice boost when legendary actress Lillian Russell, appearing in a play at Portland's Jefferson Theater in December, made her nightly appearance on stage in an Olds. Two other respected makes, the Locomobile and the Selden, joined the team in 1909.

Nickerson moved his service and storage operation to 79-85 Preble Street, into what he termed "The Largest And Best Appointed Concrete Fire Proof Garage In The State Of Maine," in May 1911. *The Sunday Telegram* went a step further: they termed Nick's new facility "One of the best equipped automobile hospitals in the State." The showroom remained under the Lafayette.

Nickerson's "automobile hospital" proved too worthy a structure: the Federal government took control of it for military manufacturing purposes during World War I, causing Nickerson to move to 37-39 Forest Avenue.

In December 1925 control of his company passed out of Nick's hand. And, in May of 1927, it was announced that the F.A. Nickerson Company would no longer exist. The new name would be the Litch-Tague Company; its new location, 832 Congress Street. About the only ingredient that remained unchanged was the automobile that was to be sold. It was the Pierce-Arrow.

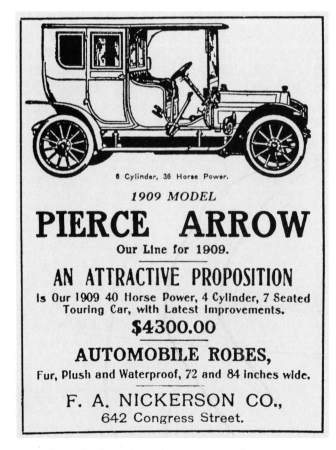

6 Cylinder, 36 Horse Power.

1909 MODEL

PIERCE ARROW
Our Line for 1909.

AN ATTRACTIVE PROPOSITION
Is Our 1909 40 Horse Power, 4 Cylinder, 7 Seated Touring Car, with Latest Improvements.

$4300.00

AUTOMOBILE ROBES,
Fur, Plush and Waterproof, 72 and 84 inches wide.

F. A. NICKERSON CO.,
642 Congress Street.

Ad, *Portland Sunday Telegram*, November 22, 1908

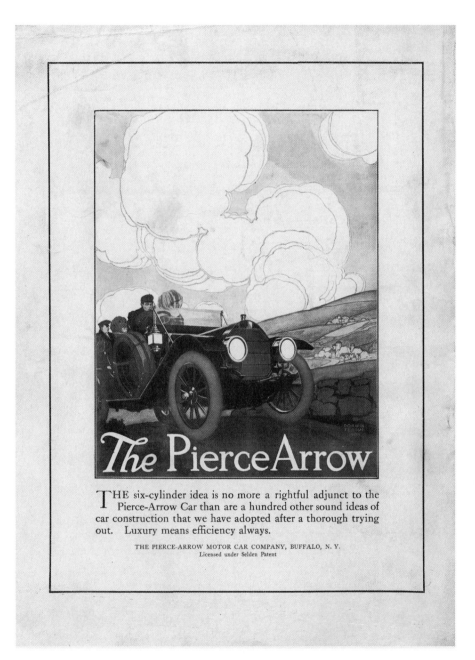

Ad, *The Horseless Age* magazine, May 11, 1910

THE PIERCE-ARROW

Evolving out of a Buffalo, New York bird cage and ice box manufacturer named Heintz, Pierce and Munschauer, the George N. Pierce Co. (later the Pierce-Arrow Motor Car Co.) went on to create, in the words of the STANDARD CATALOG, "one of the most revered and prestigious motorcars ever to grace the highway." That motorcar was, of course, the Pierce-Arrow.

Manufacture of autos began in 1901 with the Pierce Motorette, a single cylinder vehicle that was perhaps more akin to a plaything than to an automobile. Bigger and better followed, however...to the point where Pierce-Arrow eventually dignified a fair share of the most upscale homes in America (including the White House under Woodrow Wilson). During Prohibition the Pierce-Arrow was a favorite of the rum-running set because of both its power and its relatively noiseless engine.

The Pierce-Arrow and luxury were virtually synonymous...with the result that sales waned considerably in the grip of the Depression. With sales having plummeted to below 200 units a year, Pierce-Arrow ceased operations in May (on May 13th, a Friday, to be exact) of 1938.

29

THE PORTLAND COMPANY
PORTLAND

Just how powerful was the lure of the automobile? The answer: so powerful that even an outfit as big and all-encompassing as The Portland Company wanted to get in on the action. Organized in 1846, The Portland Company was the largest employer in Portland for many years... so mammoth that long-time columnist Harold Boyle could write in the Portland *Evening Express* in 1978 that "The Portland Company was to Portland years ago what Ford Motor was to Detroit."

Founded to build locomotives, The Portland Company's factory at 58 Fore Street eventually also turned out cannons and gunboats, fire engines and turbines, and propellers and papermaking machinery. Amidst all that, The Portland Company was in the auto business as well. Beginning in 1908 it was agent for the Knox, an auto it touted as "The Car for State of Maine Roads." In 1910 The Portland Company doubled its line-up: added was the Brush Runabout ("Suitable for the professional man and those requiring a machine easily handled in crowded thoroughfares."). The Cole, the Paige, and the White were a trio of other makes taken on by The Company in the years 1911-1914.

Following WWI The Portland Company turned to auto repair, and used car and gasoline sales. They regularly advertised "The Best Auto Gas In Maine," and at prices that never seemed to rise above 30¢ a gallon.

Even the all-powerful, however, can come upon hard times. By the 1970s The Portland Company was hurting. And, despite gallant efforts on the part of successful Scarborough businessman Phineas Sprague, the 136-year old firm failed in 1982.

Ad, *Portland Sunday Telegram*, December 13, 1908

30

Ad, *New England Automobile Journal*, October 22, 1910

KNOX

Pioneer auto makers not only had to worry about producing a car that would hold together... they had to worry about a sales and distribution system, too. "Live wire" agents - as Knox, here advertising in an October 1910 trade journal of the day, well knew - were a necessity in order to survive.

The Knox, named after company founder Harry A. Knox, was manufactured by the Knox Automobile Company, located in Springfield, Massachusetts. Beginning with but 15 units turned out in 1900, production rose to a high of 1412 units in 1910. The last Knox was produced in 1914.

BLAISDELL AUTOMOBILE COMPANY DEXTER

Oakland native E.D.(Ernest Dennison) Blaisdell was so enthused about the possibilities of the auto that he dropped out of the University of Maine after his junior year to form the Blaisdell Automobile Company. That was 1905. Blaisdell chose Dexter as a likely spot... but ended up with branches in Belfast and Rockland, and later Greenville, Dover-Foxcroft, Guilford, Milo, Pittsfield, and Newport as well.

Blaisdell's first location was on Grove Street. Maxwell, Ford, Buick and Overland were sold. Business boomed and in 1911 Blaisdell moved to larger space on Spring Street. E.D. liked to herald this new operation as the "Largest and Best Equipped Garage and Machine Shop in Eastern Maine." For many years an "auto show" (open house) was held in the Blaisdell showroom, complete with live music, refreshments, and decorations ("Bunting borders the entrance and festoons the main building, while the several columns of the garage, with a successful grouping of palms, are draped with white bunting and garlands of artificial roses." /*The Eastern Gazette*, February 13, 1913).

By 1922 business demanded yet additional space, and Blaisdell's Spring Street facility was doubled in size. By then Chevrolet and Hudson were the featured autos.

E.D. Blaisdell died of a heart attack at the young age of 48 in February 1931. The company that bore his name, selling Dodge as well as Hudson, continued on until 1938.

Circa 1908 postcard view of E.D. Blaisdell's original location on Grove Street, courtesy of Peter D. Bachelder, Ellsworth

Circa 1911 photo of Blaisdell's new Spring Street location, courtesy Dexter Historical Society, Dexter

Circa 1923 photo showing employees spiffed up for the Annual Employee Photo, courtesy Dexter Historical Society, Dexter

BATH AUTOMOBILE & GAS ENGINE CO.
BATH

Bath's first auto dealer was Fish & Furber, who sold Ramblers at 247 Water Street as early as 1903. But Bath Automobile & Gas Engine was a close second, starting up in April 1904. And starting up in a big way: co-proprietor was Edward W. Hyde, president of Bath Iron Works, president of the First National Bank, and Mayor of the City of Bath. An opening ad in the *Bath Daily Times* read "Demonstrations given with our Northern Runabout at any time" / "Open Tuesday, Thursday and Saturday Evenings." In addition to the Northern (manufactured in Detroit from 1902 to 1908), Bath Auto & Gas Engine carried, along the way, Pope-Tribune, Peerless, Stevens-Duryea, Chalmers, Pope-Hartford, Paige-Detroit, Cadillac ("Buy A Cadillac Runabout And Save Repairs"), E-M-F, Packard, Winton, Franklin, Elmore, Studebaker, and Dodge. Plus gas: a February 1909 ad touts "Gasolene for 13¢ a Gallon." (Ed. note: "Gasolene" is an old-fashioned variation of "Gasoline").

Located at first at 29 Centre Street and later at 13-15 Broad Street, Bath Auto & Gas Engine folded in the the summer of 1917 after losing both its Studebaker and Dodge franchises.

Ad, *Bath Daily Times*,
February 16, 1909

PEERLESS

From clothes wringers to bicycles to a highly respected automobile: such was the story of Peerless. Originally named the Peerless Manufacturing Co., the firm changed its name to the Peerless Motor Car Co. in 1902. Cleveland was always home. In 1904 the company hired world-famous racetrack driver Barney Oldfield and Barney, in a Peerless Green Dragon, spread the fame of Peerless far and wide. Soon thereafter the wonderful "All That The Name Implies" was adopted as the car's slogan.

Peerless, which peaked with 10,437 units produced in 1927, remained a formidable force until the Depression. Output came to an end in 1931. The company later became the Brewing Corp. of America, brewers of Carlings Beer and Ale.

35

WASHBURN GARAGE
BATH

This may well be the oldest-surviving automobile "station" in the State of Maine. It was constructed in 1907 by Harry Washburn, a Bath machinist who saw that the future belonged to the auto. His show-room - he sold Locomobile and Columbia - was on the ground floor; servicing was handled on the second.

In 1914 Harry Washburn gave up his garage/show-room, electing instead to repair cars out of his house at 120 North Street. The facility he'd built, though, continued on, seeing service as the Central Garage, People's Garage (Olds and International Truck), and Cummings Ford. It still stands proud today, home to Bath Fuel Co. and BFC Marine. Ask Howard Kirkpatrick, Sr. or Jr. (Howard, Sr.'s father, Samuel H. Kirkpatrick, bought the building in 1935 for $5,000!) to give you "the tour." They enjoy it. (Ed. note: built of form-poured concrete on pilings that go down to bedrock, the Washburn Garage, located at Commercial and Broad streets, was built to last forever. Howard, Sr. will laugh and tell you it's the "best place in town to be in a tornado or bombing." To see what it looks like nowadays, please turn to page 163.).

Circa 1909 postcard view, courtesy Maine Historic Preservation Commission, Augusta. Incidentally, on the address side of this postcard it reads: "American Machines For American People on American Roads."

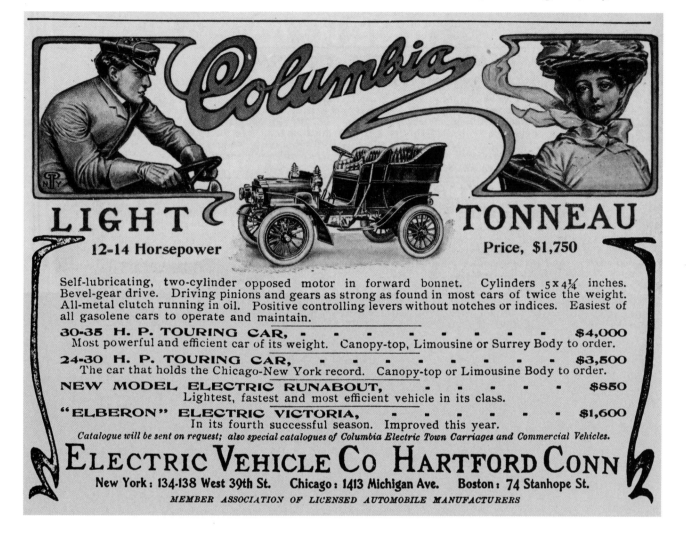

COLUMBIA

The Columbia was part of the empire of Colonel Albert A. Pope, an early auto (and bicycle) magnate whose factories extended to Toledo and Indianapolis and Hagerstown, Maryland as well as Hartford, where the Columbia was manufactured from 1897 to 1913.

"STEPHENS' SECOND ANNUAL AUTO SHOW"

While making my way through long past issues of *The Rumford Falls Times* in the Rumford library I came across a gold mine - by research standards - in the form of the complete story behind the photo shown here. The photo is from a stereoscopic view card in the collection of the Maine Historic Preservation Commission. The view was known to be of J.E. Stephens' showroom and to be from the early 1900s. But that's all that was known. So I got excited when there, on the front page of the *Times* for April 29, 1911, was the *very same* view under the headline "Stephens' Second Annual Auto Show." (Ed. note: the headline, more accurately, should have read "Stephens' Second Annual Open House," for that's what J.E. Stephens, Rumford's pioneer auto dealer, actually held.). And a two-day affair it was, with music and "pinks presented to the ladies."

Emoted the *Times'* reporter: "In the elegant garage everything was delightful to the eye. The walls were decorated with lilies and green crepe paper; many incandescents made the light as plain as day; the handsome display of Reo and Maxwell cars; the inspiring music of the Rumford band of 30 men: all these features made the evening one long to be remembered."

At least 1000 people visited the Stephens' "ware-room" (we'd call it a showroom today) during the two-day gala.

It should be mentioned that *The Rumford Falls Times'* scribe touted J.E. Stephens almost as much as his show: "Mr. Stephens is a hustler. He started out to sell 52 autos this season, and some of the local agents laughed at his expectations. But the season has just opened and Mr. Stephens has to date sold 16 cars." (Ed. note: J.E. far exceeded his sales goal. By October he was at 69 and still counting.).

Stereoscopic view card, April 1911, courtesy Maine Historic Preservation Commission, Augusta

Ad, *THE NUNTIUS*, magazine of Canton High School, Canton, March 1916

J.E. STEPHENS RUMFORD

The late Rumford historian Stuart Martin termed John E. Stephens "the first dealer in automobiles in Oxford County." There's no doubt about that: Stephens, born in West Paris in 1859 and a highly successful Rumford jewelry and sporting goods merchant, sold his first autos at his garage/showroom on Canal Street away back in 1904. He started with Ramblers and the Stevens-Duryea; later switched to Reo and Maxwell. Of note: if you purchased a car from J.E. Stephens you might well find your name in one of his ads. An April 15, 1911 ad, for example, lists as recent customers: "Chester Bisbee, Rumford Falls, Maxwell" and "A Dixfield man, Reo Touring Car."

Stephens replaced Maxwell with Dodge circa 1915. He went out of the auto business in 1920, involving himself thereafter in civic welfare. The former Stephens High School (Rumford's high school until 1968) was named in John E. Stephens' honor. He died in Rumford, at age 80, in December 1939.

MILES B. MANK MOTOR CAR COMPANY PORTLAND

Warren native Miles B. Mank had Cadillac blood flowing through his veins. After service with Cadillac in the midwest and southern New England, he became co-proprietor, with George L. Stuart, of Mank-Stuart Motor Car Company, 17-21 Forest Avenue, in November 1909. In November 1910 the partners enlarged to where they occupied 9-21 Forest (the cleanliness of which so impressed a *Sunday Telegram*

CADILLAC

Cadillac was named for Le Sieur Antoine de la Mothe Cadillac, a Frenchman who, in the early 1700s, explored the site of present-day Detroit. First manufactured in the fall of 1902, Cadillac was known as an auto of refinement right from its very beginning. It became part of General Motors in 1909; has been the jewel of GM ever since.

A Wonderful Car Which Is Creating a Veritable Sensation From the Atlantic to the Pacific

MILES B. MANK MOTOR CAR CO.
9-13 Forest Avenue

reporter that he scribed "Silk dresses need have no fear of this place."). Less than a year later, in August 1912, Mank bought out Stuart and became the Miles B. Mank Motor Car Company. Ever on the move, Mank had a brand new facility constructed where once stood the old Forest Avenue Baseball Grounds, at 343-349 Forest Avenue. Opened in February 1917, the facility was said to be "one of the finest of its kind east of Boston... and better than a great many now used in the Hub." Costs were estimated at "about $40,000."

Miles B. Mank eventually strayed from selling only Cadillac. In 1917 he added the Detroit Electric; in 1918 the Fulton Truck. Another move, to 79-85 Preble Street (F. A. Nickerson's old haunt), was made in late 1919. In October 1921 Mank ceased to represent Cadillac. He relocated to 188 State Street, where he took on the sale of a competing luxury car, the Marmon. Miles B. Mank made one last move, to 73-75 Preble, in June 1922, and took on the sale of one last "machine," the Rollin (produced only in 1924-1925), in February 1924. He gave up his own dealership later that same year, but remained active in the auto world as a vice-president of the Maine Automobile Association. He died in February 1959 at age 90.

Circa 1910 photo, courtesy Collections of the Maine Historical Society, Portland

1911

1910

"Autos Getting To Look Much Alike" headlined an article in the Portland *Evening Express*. (January)

It was estimated that Detroit would produce 60% of all cars made in the U.S. in 1910. (February)

The number of automobiles registered in Maine approached the 5,000 mark. (February)

Kate Douglas Wiggin, "the noted authoress," purchased a Chalmers-Detroit touring car from the Harmon Automobile Co. of Portland. (March)

Motorists were warned not to drive at night unless "the steering wheel is capable, the brakes effective, and the lighting is eminently satisfactory for the purpose." (March)

President Taft visited Bangor and enjoyed a tour of the city by auto. (May)

On Sunday July 10th the one-day auto crossing record for the Piscataqua River Bridge was broken "with the passage of 400 machines between Maine and New Hampshire." (July)

C.W. Post, the Michigan cereal man, visited Portland in his $10,000 Pierce-Arrow touring sedan. (August)

It was recommended, in a *Sunday Telegram* article, that motorists who suffer from cold feet should try "removing part of the footboard and allowing the hot air from the engine to circulate around their feet." (December)

1911

"Motor Cars a Source of Much Revenue to the State of Maine" headlined a *Sunday Telegram* account, reporting that $10,724 was collected in license and registration fees in 1910. (January)

President John N. Willys of the Willys-Overland Co. stated the auto industry had reached the point of "survival of the fittest," predicting that "scores of fly-by-night and mushroom concerns" would soon fail. (September)

The Portland *Evening Express* declared Old Orchard Beach and Orlando, Florida the two greatest automobile racing beaches in America. (September)

Hudson joined several other manufacturers in equipping their new models with self-starters. (October)

The auto, by allowing easier access to and from the city, was labeled a "suburb builder." (October)

"I can't stand the toot of an automobile horn."

"How's that?"

"A fellow eloped with my wife in an automobile, and every time I hear a horn toot I think he's bringing her back."

Sunday Telegram (October)

To William L. Hayford of Bucksport went the honor of registering the 10,000th car in Maine, a gas-powered, 25-horse power touring car. (October)

1912

Doctors are far and away the most prolific users of the automobile, stated an article in the *Sunday Telegram*. The need for reliable transportation was cited as the reason. (February)

A "refrigerette" - consisting of two trays, one for ice and beverages and one for food and snacks - was said to be the latest in truly up-to-date autos. (March)

The newly-passed Maine Automobile Law called for a top speed of 25 miles-per-hour in the country and 10 in the built-up sections of towns and cities. Speed at all times had to be "reasonable and safe." (March)

The Rochester Fair, in Rochester, N.H., featured an Automobile Day. Included in the Day was an Automobile Slow Race in High Gear ($175.00 in prizes) and an Automobile Race of Decorated Cars ($185.00 in prizes). (September)

Red Sox fans presented a White "30" Roadster to Sox manager Jake Stahl in appreciation of his guiding the Bosox to the American League flag. (Ed. note: the team's catcher in over half of its games that year was Lewiston's own Bill Carrigan). Said Jake: "The car is a beauty and I know it will meet every demand that I can put on it." (October)

New York, with 83,000, and California, with 61,784, led the nation in terms of autos in active use. Maine chimed in at 10,056.

1913

It was predicted the new sport of auto polo (played with a basketball and one stripped down car, a driver, and a mallet man vs. a second stripped down car, driver, and mallet man) might well "take its place among the thrilling sports." (February)

The New York Sun compared the selection of a car to the selection of a marriage partner, concluding "It is not the less important that car and owner should be compatible in temper than it is with the man who picks out the girl he would like to marry and proposes to her." (April)

Following the lead of a California concern, a Detroit company opened a "laundry" for autos. The process took 20 minutes and the company's slogan was "Everything back but the dirt!" (May)

L.S. Schlosberg, 591 Congress Street, Portland, advertised "The Smartest Motor Coats East Of Boston." (July)

The *Sunday Telegram* featured a map of the Lincoln Highway, the nation's first transcontinental highway. (September)

1914

There were 145 auto manufacturers, producing a total of 242 chassis models, in operation in the U.S. The average price of a new car was $2,347.00. (February)

The Charles M. Hay Co., 8-12 Free Street, Portland, advertised gas at 17¢ a gallon. (April)

A moose charged an automobile along a lonely stretch of nighttime road at Fort Fairfield. It was the first recorded instance of such an attack, and north country motorists were advised not to drive at night as "the headlights act on moose and deer in the same manner as a jack light," attracting them. (September)

At year's end there were an estimated 1,666,984 pleasure vehicles registered in the U.S., with Maine having 15,065 of them. (December)

1915

In the largest single auto transaction to date, the Allies purchased 25,000 Ford touring cars for use in troop deployment in Europe. (January)

"America's Sweetheart," Mary Pickford, purchased a Maxwell cabriolet. Miss Pickford was said to be an expert driver and to be enthused about the car. (March)

A New York Overland dealer erected a huge Overland sign at the Polo Grounds (home of the New York Giants), 394 feet from home plate, and offered a free Overland to the first Giant player to hit the sign on the fly. (June)

Automobile races were one of the major features at the Maine State Fair, in Lewiston. Promised were

"The highest powered cars and fastest drivers in the Country." (July)

Our national anthem? Why it is "My auto 'tis of thee, short cut to poverty - of thee I chant," or something like that, isn't it?

Portland *Evening Express* (July)

President Wilson was in an auto accident while touring the New Hampshire countryside near Newport. The president and his party were shaken up but no one was hurt. (July)

Fresno, California adopted the Honor System. Signs read "Motorists attention! You are on your honor. Fresno County has no speed cops. Drive so they will not be needed. Speed limit 30 miles per hour." Other locales were said to be considering adopting the system as well. (August)

The Ford Motor Co. mailed $50.00 rebate checks to the more than 300,000 persons who had purchased a Ford between August 1914 and August 1915. (September)

1916

The first car registered in Maine for 1916 was a Willys-Knight belonging to Governor Oakley Curtis. (January)

Lady: "And you say you're an educated man?"

Tramp: "Yes, Mum, I'm a roads scholar."

The Racquet, magazine of Portland High School (February)

With wartime shortages taking their toll, Russia announced it had found a way to make tires from vodka. (April)

Stalled Motorist: "My boy, I hope that is gasoline you have in that jug."

Native Boy: "Gee! I hope it ain't...it'd taste like the dickens on my pancakes!"

The Oracle, the magazine of Bangor High School (June)

The Clark St. Garage, 97-101 Clark Street, Portland, advertised cars washed for 75¢. Included in the ad was the promise "Extra Good Job." (October)

There were an even dozen auto dealerships on lower Forest Avenue in Portland along what would soon become known as "Auto Row." (December)

1917

Former Red Sox and White Sox star thirdbaseman - and Porter, Maine native - Harry Lord bought a Buick touring car from pioneer Buick dealer Wm. B. Thombs of Portland. (And the *Sunday Telegram* scribe who reported this bit of news couldn't resist adding: "Evidently Harry feels that no matter how far he journeys, if he rides in a Buick he will be able to make a home run at any time he chooses.") (February)

The United States declared war against Germany. (April)

The employees of the Franklin Automobile Co., Syracuse, New York, showed their patriotic colors by raising the funds to buy and display fully 1,000 American flags in and around their factory. (May)

Ford was said to be manufacturing 200,000 airplane cylinders as a part of the American war effort. (September)

General John "Black Jack" Pershing chose a Hudson Super Six phaeton as his command car in France. (September)

1918

An automobile - a Ford carrying three passengers - was driven across the frozen waters of Penobscot Bay...the first time such a feat was accomplished. (March)

The citizens of Berlin, New Hampshire considered changing their town's name. (May)

Montford S. Hill, chief clerk in Maine's automobile bureau, stated that he thought people should have to pass some kind of driving test before being allowed to register their car. (June)

"Because of the manner in which some automobilists speed their cars," reported the *Biddeford Daily Journal*, Saco officials passed an ordinance restricting the speed limit to 15 miles per hour within their city's limits. (July)

New York, with 434,006, and California, with

311,619, led the nation in autos registered. Maine came in at 46,875. (November)

"THE BOYS ARE COMING BACK" ran an ad happily paid for by Portland's Hudson dealer, Henley-Kimball. It said it all: the War was over! (November)

1919

Portland's Charles M. Hay Co. advertised a kit with which an auto owner could repaint his/her car, in a choice of 12 colors, for $4.25. Black was $4.00. Sandpaper and brushes were included. (March)

Wallace Reid starred in the motion picture *The Roaring Road*, described as "A Five Act Fast Moving Story of An Even Faster Automobile Salesman." (April)

Student: "Did the Romans have automobiles?"

Teacher: "No. Why do you ask?"

Student: "Well, it says here that they crossed the Rubicon by fords."

> *The Oracle*, **magazine of Bangor High School (June)**

Dickson's Garage, 10 York Street, Portland, advertised auto repair labor rates of $1.00 an hour. (September)

It was reported that 20 auto makers were now equipping at least some of their new models with heaters. (November)

1917

STOUGHTON-FOLKINS
PORTLAND

Stoughton-Folkins made its debut in January 1907. Proprietors were Peter T. Stoughton and Murray S. Folkins. Their location was 222-224 Commercial Street; their stock in trade the "celebrated Maxwell."

In January 1909 the partners moved to 68 Oak Street, converting a former stable into what they named the Central Garage. Wrote the *Portland Sunday Telegram*: "The interior of the building on the ground floor has been entirely changed for their convenience. The floor is of concrete and new windows have been put in to give better light. There is a display room for the Maxwell cars and the business offices are located near the display room. The building is brightly lighted with a large number of electric lights and heated throughout by steam." Further noted the *Telegram's* reporter: "Lavatories and toilets have also been installed for the convenience of the employees and patrons."

In December 1909 the partners added Oldsmobile and Oakland to their line-up, followed by Rambler in February 1910.

In May 1911 Murray Folkins went out on his own, setting up at 779 (later 685) Forest Avenue and handling Hupmobiles. Stoughton-Folkins, however, continued on. The firm moved to larger quarters - "The largest one floor space of any Garage in the City" - at 82-88 Oak Street in December 1913. Within two years, however, Peter Stoughton began to wind down. He sublet a large chunk of his garage to E.R. Bensons's Studebaker sales and service, preferring Stoughton-Folkins focus on repairs and tire/auto supply business. And so it did, until 1938. That's the year Peter Stoughton retired and Stoughton-Folkins ceased to exist.

Ad, program, U.C.T. Minstrels, Portland, February 1914

OAKLAND 30 H. P. $1,000

Thousands of Oaklands are in use in the hands of salesmen who require continuous service; ask any of them about Oakland and they will invariably say, "the best car built."

OTHER MODELS $1,075 TO $3,000

STOUGHTON-FOLKINS CO. 68 OAK STREET.

Ad, *The Literary Digest*, August 17, 1929

OAKLAND

The Oakland is still with us today. Sort of. It was launched in Pontiac, Michigan in 1907-1908 by partners Edward M. Murphy and Alanson P. Brush. Neither was a stranger to the world of transportation. Murphy owned the Pontiac Buggy Company; Brush had been involved in the design of the Cadillac. Their creation was named "Oakland" because that's what Murphy called his successful line of buggies.

Brush departed the partnership early-on, and Murphy died suddenly, at age 44, in September 1909. By then, though, Oakland had become a part of General Motors' fledgling empire.

Oakland remained in the GM line-up for the better part of two and a half decades. Its undoing was the birth of the Pontiac - originally an Oakland model - in 1926. Pontiac, described in the *STANDARD CATALOG* as "a quality six (cylinder) sold at a four's price," was a smash success, outselling its "parent" hands down.

In 1931, with the Depression in full sway and Oakland sales less than overwhelming, GM hierarchy called an end to the line. The next year, 1932, they went one step further: they changed the name of the Oakland Motor Car Company to the Pontiac Motor Car Company.

SEVERANCE & CRAIG
BANGOR

Partnerships come. And partnerships go. But the partnership of Percy E. Severance and J. Arthur Craig barely even had a chance to settle. The two – Severance was a dry goods merchant and Craig an inveterate salesman – came together at 27 Franklin Street in February 1913, just in time to exhibit at Bangor's very first Auto Show. The duo handled Maxwell, Metz, Rambler, Cross Country (a Rambler product) and International Harvester trucks. A May 1913 *Bangor Daily News'* ad read: "Come in and look them (the duo's auto selection) over and if interested, have a demonstration." It would appear few people took them up on their offer: within less than a year the partnership of Severance & Craig was history.

Photo, 1913. But is it Severance or is it Craig doing the honors outside their short-lived establishment? Courtesy of Blanche B. Martin, Bangor

Ad, *Success* magazine,
May 1904

RAMBLER

Rambler could trace its heritage back to the late 1800s. At first a successful make of bicycle, its name began adorning the automobile in 1897, the brainchild of Thomas B. Jeffrey. Produced initially in Chicago, but primarily in Kenosha, Wisconsin, the Rambler was manufactured until 1913. It later enjoyed a second life as a Nash/American Motors' product in the 1950s.

DARLING AUTOMOBILE CO.
AUBURN (AND PORTLAND, BANGOR, AUGUSTA)

The best known name in Maine auto annals is almost assuredly "Darling." You may thank V. (Veranus) S. Darling for that. Born in West Baldwin, Maine in 1876, Darling sold bicycles and sporting goods in Auburn before the coming of the car. From 1903 on, though, he concentrated on selling autos. He handled the Crestmobile (made in Cambridge, Mass.), Buick, Maxwell, Hudson, Olds, others... and liked to run small ads that read "Cars Of Quality Sell On Their Merits... Not Large Ads." It was Reo, however, that was V.S.'s favorite. The Darling Automobile Co. sold lots of Reos. And, although he did a banner business in Auburn at the huge 29-31 Turner Street facility pictured here, Darling wasn't content. He established a sizable branch in Portland in 1911, all the better to sell Reos. A May 1915 Sunday Telegram clip stated that, because of V.S. Darling, "Maine is certainly a Reo State." By 1922 the Darling Automobile Co. was selling upwards of a million dollars worth of Reos a year.

Veranus S. Darling unfortunately died in Auburn in January 1942 from Bright's Disease. But the business he had so well established continued to roll. A branch was opened in Bangor in December 1926; one in Augusta shortly thereafter.

The Darling Automobile Co. sold its last Reo Flying Cloud and closed its doors in Auburn in July 1935. The Darling name in Portland and Augusta is history, too. But distant relative John Darling has kept the union of "Darling" and "Automobile" very much alive, with two present-day facilities in Bangor and one in Ellsworth.

Postcard view, 1914. (Note how the sender "personalized" the card!).

Ad, program for The Bluffers, Senior Drama, Edward Little High School, Auburn, April 1923

REO

Ransom E. Olds was quite the auto pioneer. After designing the car, Oldsmobile (please see page 103), that yet bears his name, he went out and designed another winner, the Reo (as in <u>R</u>ansom <u>E</u>. <u>O</u>lds). The first Reo was introduced in late 1905, and was a big success at the Madison Square Garden Auto Show in January 1906. For the thirty years after that Reo was a highly respected name. The Depression eventually did Reo's auto business in, however. The last Reo auto (the company continued to make trucks) left its Lansing, Michigan plant in 1936.

R.A. PARTRIDGE
LEWISTON

Born in Belgrade, Maine in 1875, Roland A. Partridge was well into his adult years when he got into the auto business in Lewiston. That was 1910, the year he and Arthur W. Nelke opened their Central Garage at 224 Main Street. Before another year had passed the partners had opened up a second location, too, at 88-90 Bates Street. By 1913 Partridge was on his own at 88-90 Bates. The Winton, a highly successful car of its day, appears to be his first new car venture. In 1916 Partridge added a new partner, Chester R. Farris, and they took on the Willys-Overland line. A July 1916 Partridge & Farris ad touts the Overland as "The World's Most Powerful Low Priced Car." The very next month, though, Partridge was back on his own. A large *Lewiston Evening Journal* ad of August 19th announced that Mr. R.A. Partridge was now head of Hudson Motor Sales Company (located at 286 Main, but soon moved to the more familiar 88-90 Bates address).

Roland Partridge headed up the local Hudson operation - adding Oakland in 1919 - until 1921, when he began a battery sales outlet in partnership with one Alvin Mitchell at 207 Middle Street. He later worked at Plummer & Merrill, morticians. He died in Auburn in 1949.

Ad, program, Maine State Fair, Lewiston, September 1914

WINTON SIX THE CAR THAT PUT SIXES ON THE MAP

REMEMBER, ALL STATEMENTS MADE IN WINTON ADVERTISING ARE TRUE WITHOUT QUALIFICATION

DID it ever occur to you where the six cylinder industry was founded? Who was the first designer and builder of a motor car to equip his car with a self cranking device, a full floating rear axle and cast aside the inferior four, and manufacture the superior six exclusively? Alexander Winton is the answer to all these questions.

The Winton Motor Car Company are today the only manufacturers of high grade pleasure cars, that are conducting business under the same head as when founded.

A manufacturer who jumps from the four to a six and then back to the four, is merely experimenting and is not producing a proven product. The Winton Six holds the World's record for upkeep expense—25.1 cent per thousand miles. A contest among car owners and drivers, that no other manufacturer has cared to attempt. Compare the Winton Six selling at $3250 with anything under $4000, if you find a car any better, can you state in what way it is superior?

The 1914 WINTON SIX includes in its equipment, a Mohair Top, Clear Vision Windshield, Gray & Davis Electric Lighting System, Warner Speedometer and Clock Combination, Kellogg Air Pump, and German Silver Radiator with Metal Parts Nickled

R. A. PARTRIDGE
STATE OF MAINE AGENT
88 Bates Street   Lewiston, Maine
TELEPHONE CONNECTION

WINTON SIX

Smart and Graceful

Victoria
Sedan
Town Car
Limousine

THO the closed car is always in season, it is particularly essential after summer passes. Winton Six closed cars are especially noteworthy this fall. Our surprising new motor makes them as fleet and graceful in action as they are smart and appealing in design. Whether you prefer victoria, sedan, town car or limousine, you will find your ideal awaiting you in a Winton Six closed car. Insure early delivery by booking your order promptly. May we send you literature?

The Winton Company
82 Berea Road, Cleveland, O.. U. S. A.

Ad, *Motor* magazine, December 1919

WINTON

A native of Scotland who emigrated to Cleveland in 1884, Alexander Winton became a success in the bicycle-manufacturing business. He then turned to cars, organizing the Winton Motor Carriage Co. (later The Winton Company) in 1897, and producing "Smart and Graceful" automobiles until financial difficulties caused production to cease in 1924.

Photos, 1915. Both courtesy of McArthur Public Library, Biddeford

HARMON'S CENTRAL GARAGE
BIDDEFORD

Which would you rather be? An auto dealer? Or a school principal? Ernest L. Harmon was both. Born in Biddeford in 1882, Harmon graduated from Biddeford High and, by 1907, was principal of his hometown's Summer Street Grammar School. Next, circa 1912, came partnership with

Roy V. Ross in a garage/auto dealership known as Harmon & Ross at 39 Washington Street. They sold the Jackson. (See page 23). They also did repairs, sold auto supplies and, by June 1913, could advertise "We have a concrete wash stand and can wash your car at short notice."

By 1915 Harmon and Ross had split up. Ross opened the Roy V. Ross Garage at Pepperell Square in Saco. Harmon remained at 39 Washington but changed the name of his endeavor to the Central Garage (it was next door to the Central Fire Station) and traded Jackson for Dodge.

Ernest L. Harmon ran a garage and sold autos until 1926. He later, from 1931 to 1936, served Biddeford as Postmaster. During World War II he assumed the post of Chairman of the Biddeford-Saco Rationing Board. He died in 1966.

Ad, *Portland Sunday Telegram,*
February 20, 1916

E.R BENSON
PORTLAND

Portland played host to a plenitude of Studebaker dealers through the years. My best count comes in at an even dozen. E. (Ernest) R. Benson was not the first - that honor goes to one J.B. Soule, who opened at 891 Congress Street in 1912 - but he was almost certainly the most impressive. Credentials included a stint as National Sales Manager for Cadillac, followed by three years as V.P./Sales for Studebaker. So why not now "Studebakerize" Portland (and, for that matter, all of Maine and northern New Hampshire, too... for it was all included in Benson's territory) he must have reasoned. The answer: because Portland (and, for that matter, all of Maine and northern New Hampshire, too) weren't ready to be "Studebakerized." Sure, Benson set up a hefty assortment of better than 20 associate dealers that stretched from Presque Isle, Calais, and Winn to Rumford, and Berlin and Somersworth, New Hampshire. But it wasn't enough. Ford and GM and the rest had other plans. The result: in spite of his many credentials, E.R. Benson does not appear to have made much of a dent in the northern New England motor car market. He began in Portland, first at 88 Oak Street and then at 345 Cumberland Avenue. By the spring of 1918, though, he was gone... and Jordan & York had taken over E.R.'s old showroom at 345 Cumberland and had become the new kids on the Studebaker block.

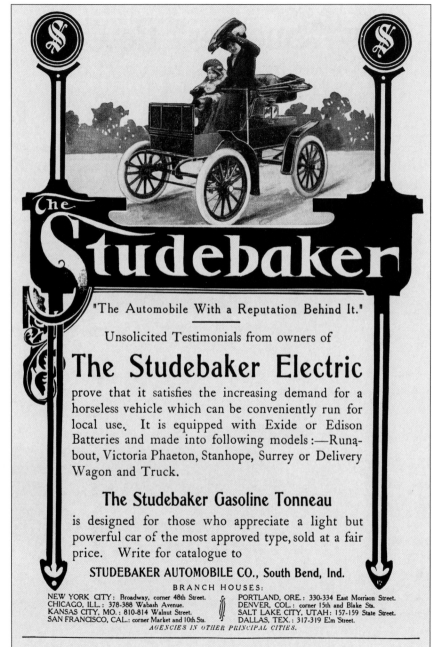

Ad, *Success* magazine, May 1904

STUDEBAKER ELECTRIC

Highly successful in the wagon-manufacturing business, the Studebaker brothers were not overly eager to involve themselves in the automobile-manufacturing business. But they did, in 1902, with an electric vehicle developed for them by none other than Thomas Alva Edison. Studebaker entered the gasoline auto market in 1904, but continued to produce electrics, in limited quantities, until 1912. (Ed. note: for more on Studebaker please see page 101).

CENTRAL GARAGE
BRIDGTON

The Central Garage was constructed in 1913 as Washburn & Callamore's Central Garage. Its arrival was part of the change in things brought about by the coming of the automobile. As Norman Libby recounted in the 1968 book, HISTORY OF BRIDGTON, MAINE: "Up to this time the farmers took half a day and came up to the bank to deposit their money. With the automobile, they took an hour, went to the bank and borrowed money to take home to run the farm."

The Central Garage, which sold and serviced Dodge, passed into the ownership of R. Everett Starrett and Clarence Turner, Jr. in 1915. Then a strange event occurred. On October 14, 1916 Starrett and his wife journeyed to Portland. It was their second wedding anniversary. Starrett took leave of his wife to conduct some business at a garage on Forest Avenue, completed the business, boarded a trolley to rejoin his wife downtown... and was never seen or heard from again. He, wrote the *Evening Express* on the front page of its October 16th edition, "disappeared as completely as though the earth had opened and swallowed him." To this day, no trace of R. Everett Starrett has ever been found.

Clarence Turner, Jr. operated the Central Garage with new partner G.C Wolf until 1918. Then Wolf operated it on his own through 1919, when the garage was purchased by Ripley & Fletcher (q.v.) and run by them as a Ford dealership. The structure was later utilized by the town of Bridgton as a storage depot for its plows and road equipment.

STOP AT
CENTRAL GARAGE
BRIDGTON, MAINE
Everything you would expect to find in a real garage---and then some
Agents for the famous
Dodge Brothers
MOTOR CAR
Batavia, Republic and Goodrich Auto Tires always on hand
Our Motto — "Satisfaction First and Always."

It Speaks for Itself
Complete Machine Shop
Vulcanizing of Tubes and Caseings
Storage and Gasolene
R. E. STARRETT   C. E. TURNER, JR.

R. Everett Starrett in a 1916 photo. If Mr. Starrett were to suddenly reappear after all these years what do you suppose he'd make of today's automobile scene?

Main St., Bridgton, Me.

CENTRAL GARAGE

Circa 1915 postcard view

59

RUMFORD GARAGE
RUMFORD

"The Largest and Best Equipped Garage in Oxford County": so read ads in *The Rumford Falls Times* of February 1912, just after the garage had opened for business. Proprietor George W. Pettengill wasn't bashful about his new car sales designs, either. If you purchased a new Hudson, E-M-F, or Flanders, Pettengill promised to "keep it in condition" absolutely free for a full year.

By 1915 Studebaker (which took over E-M-F in 1912) and Ford - as well as Hudson - were Pettengill's cars of choice. Lincoln was later added, too.

The Rumford Garage remained in operation through 1938. Its former building, at 50 Prospect Avenue, is now home to Puiia's Home Center. George W. Pettengill died in Mattawamkeag in December 1955.

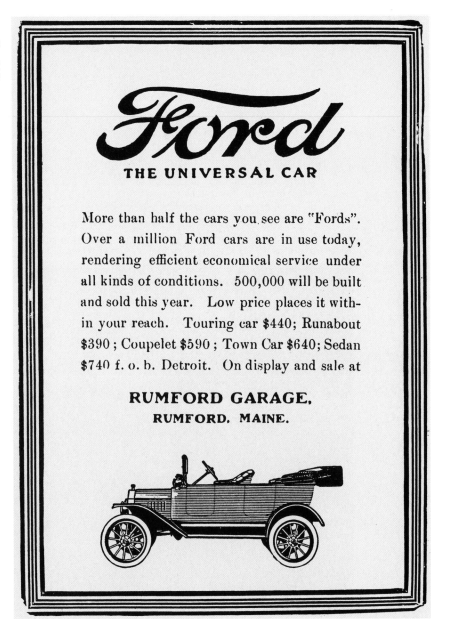

FORD BOOSTER COMIC POSTCARDS

There was a whole series of what were known as Ford Booster Comic postcards printed circa 1915. These are two I especially like.

While the Big Car simply puffs and grunts
It takes a Ford to do these stunts

The Big Car's burning up the road
Why sure! Just see by whom it's towed

CHANDLER MOTORS OF MAINE
DAMARISCOTTA

In May 1917 Chandler Motors of Maine, headquartered in Portland, converted what had been the stable building for the Royal Hall Hotel in Damriscotta into a branch auto showroom/service center. A May 20th *Sunday Telegram* column noted "The new establishment is very large and well equipped and has been attractively arranged," while a July 29th article mentioned that "The Chandler station at Damariscotta is proving a very popular place with motorists traveling eastward."

Circa 1917 postcard view

While originally called just Chandler Motors of Maine (as shown here), the operation soon took on a name of its own, the Motor Service Station. Chandler ("Famous For Its Marvelous Motor") was featured, but the Dort and the Cleveland were also sold.

In June 1927 another name change was made, to Damariscotta Garage. Later uses included being a Mobilgas station, and an appliance center. The structure, which stood at 3 Elm Street, was demolished in the 1950s. (Ed. note: the building to the left in the photo survives, and is today home to the Weatherbird Shop.).

Ad, *Motor* magazine, April 1918

CHANDLER

In 1913 a group of veteran automobile men headed by F. C. Chandler moved from Detroit to Cleveland. The result was the Chandler Motor Car Co. and a car, the Chandler, that sold as many as 20,268 units in its top year, 1926. After that top year, though, the company's fortunes - and finances - waned quickly and considerably, with the outcome being the ceasing of production just three years later, in 1929.

R.M. FLAGG
BANGOR

In 1915 Roscoe M. Flagg went from being proprietor of the Bangor Watch Co., at 36 Main Street, to being proprietor of R.M. Flagg, auto dealer, with a showroom at 33-A Park Street and a garage at 16 Bower Street. An opening year ad offers a line-up of "Inter-State, Chalmers, National Automobiles and Accessories."

Within a year Flagg had moved both his showroom, to 93-97 Central Street, and his service garage, to 329 Hammond Street. And within another year, by 1917, he'd added the Marmon to his offering of autos.

Flagg liked to bounce around. By 1920 he was at 56 Post Office Square. He'd changed names as well, to the Bangor Auto Exchange. In 1923 Flagg ceased selling cars, turning instead to heating and refrigeration equipment. He did make two additional forays into the auto field. In 1929-1931 he tried his hand with Cord and Auburn (two rather legendary automobiles, both made in Indiana). And from 1935 to 1941 he was the Bangor agent for Nash. After that it was strictly heating and electrical equipment all the way to the mid-1970s. That's when the R.M. Flagg Co. closed its doors.

Ad, *Sprague's Journal Of Maine History*, Feb./March/April 1918

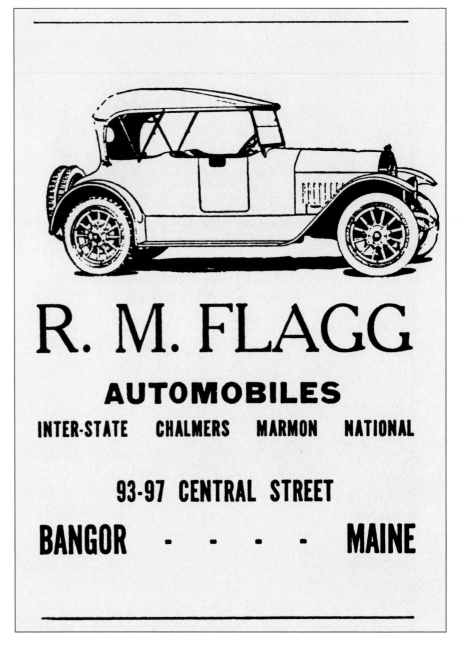

Evers—Chicago Nat.

CHALMERS

The Chalmers, produced in Detroit from 1911 to 1924, was a classy car that will forever be enshrined in baseball history. That's because the Chalmers Motor Car Co. gave birth to the idea of a Most Valuable Player award: from 1911 to 1914 the company presented a sparkling new Chalmers to the player in both leagues that the Chalmers Trophy Commission deemed most valuable. Winners, over the four-year period, were Tris Speaker, Ty Cobb, "Laughing Larry" Doyle, Walter "The Big Train" Johnson, Eddie Collins, Jake Daubert (a two-time NL batting champ now almost completely forgotten), Frank "Wildfire" Schulte (a two-time NL home run champ now truly completely forgotten), and the player pictured here, stellar Cubs' and Braves' (Boston Braves!) secondsacker Johnny Evers.

Johnny Evers as portrayed on a 1911 Mecca Cigarettes' baseball card

CARIBOU MOTOR COMPANY
CARIBOU

To the Caribou Motor Company goes the honor of being one of Maine's longest-lasting auto dealerships. It began, as S.W. Collins & Son, in early 1912. Actually, S. (Samuel) W. Collins had died in the 1880s, but his firm, big into lumbering, continued to bear his name. The "Son" was Herschel, and it was he who got the firm into selling autos. Primarily Fords. A May 1912 ad in *The Aroostook Republican* headlined "Go - go - go - a-Fording" and went on to tout the Model T as "lightest, rightest - most economical." But S.W. Collins & Son (Ed. note: S.W. was Senator Susan Collins' great, great grandfather; Herschel, her great grandfather) sold other makes, too. In May 1916 it was noted in *The Republican* that "S.W. Collins & Son have so far this season sold 21 Fords, 4 Dodges and 2 Hudsons." Not bad.

In November of 1918 Herschel sold the dealership to Willis L. Oak, a long-standing Collins' employee. Oak, in turn, sold to a trio of partners headed by E.F. Shaw in January 1921. It was Shaw, that same year, who began the use of the name Caribou Motor Company. It was a name that would last for the better part of seven decades, until E.F. Shaw's grandson, Sheldon Scott, sold the agency in 1989.

All three of the photos reproduced here are circa 1924 and are courtesy of Sheldon Scott, longtime Caribou Motor Company president. Born in 1925, Sheldon was, literally, "born" into the Caribou Motor Company, too. His grandfather was E.F. Shaw and his father and uncle were Caribou Motor men as well. Sheldon recalls going down to the dealership as a kid in the 1930s - after school, of course - and playing in the parts department. "I liked to look at the parts," he smiles. And sometimes he'd go to the train depot and "help" unload new autos as they came in.

Back to the photos, though. The shot on the facing page shows the service building when the dealership was in its original location at 15 Sweden Street. (The firm moved to 398 Main Street in 1939). The shots on this page afford a rather rare look at the inside of an early and quite sizable parts department. Caribou Motor Company was, if you'll pardon the play on Aroostook County's main claim to fame, no small potatoes!

1926

1920

A study undertaken by the B.F. Goodrich Rubber Co. predicted that there would be one auto to every two U.S. families by January 1921. (February)

The Rangeley correspondent for *The Franklin Journal* reported that "Automobiles were seen on the street Saturday, April 3." (April)

Best-selling author Sinclair Lewis, writing in *The Saturday Evening Post*, proclaimed that "Motoring is the real test of marriage: after a week together on the road you either want a divorce...or discover again the spouse you used to know." (May)

The *Sunday Telegram* helped spread the news that one Franklin Freeman, who lived on Franklin Street in the village of Franklinton in the county of Franklin, had just purchased a new Franklin car through the Franklin dealership in Franklin County, North Carolina. (July)

Mrs. Beatrice Hall McFadden of Bath enjoyed the distinction of driving an auto, a 1920 Premier, over the top of Mt. Washington. She was thought to be the first female to accomplish that formidable task. (July)

Towle's Garage, located in the Woodfords section of Portland, advertised "A New Stunt: Automobile Washing While You Wait." (August)

In a hint of what was to come, a rum-running party of three cars was intercepted in Baring, just across from Canada. Two of the cars got away but one was captured after it "turned turtle." (overturned). (October)

1921

It was reported that 90 companies, spread across 32 states (Ed. note: Maine was not one of the 32), produced 1,906,000 passengers cars in the calendar year 1920. (February)

The Portland Chamber of Commerce called upon state officials to halt the damage being done to the state highways leading into Portland by heavy trucks. (May)

A girl's idea of a wasted evening is to go out auto riding with her fellow and another couple, with her fellow doing the driving.
        The Bates Student, **magazine of Bates College, Lewiston (May)**

"Florence Harding blue," named after president Harding's wife, was widely adopted as an automobile color.

The Bangor Fair advertised that it had that "Latest Sensation," Auto Polo. (August)

In Detroit, motorists who parked illegally found their cars removed to the city pound and found themselves paying fines of $1.00 to $5.00. (October)

The Portland Co., 58 Fore Street, Portland, advertised Aero High Test Gasoline for 30¢ a gallon. (December)

1922

The Lewiston Evening Journal reported that Rumfordites were leading the way, by attaching a set of runners to the front axle of their autos...and keeping them in operation right through the snow season. (January)

The Anderson 6 (Ed. note: What a great name!) was advertised as the "Big Sensation" at Portland's Auto Show. John Graham of Old Orchard Beach was the local agent. (February)

1920-1929

It was stated that Pomeroy W. Jordan, a Cape Elizabeth farmer, had amassed a quite remarkable 143,729 miles on his Dodge Brothers auto. Mr. Jordan remarked that "the car seems to grow continually better." (March)

The American Automobile Association (AAA) held a contest to come up with the name that best described a reckless driver. The winning entry, suggested by one F.B. Simpson of Cedar Rapids, Iowa, was "Flivverboob." (June)

Charles W. Nash, head of Nash Motors Co., landed a 190-pound halibut off the Cutler coast. (November)

In San Diego, in a new plan to curb fast driving, a person convicted of speeding was made to attach a large red placard, with the word "DANGEROUS" printed in black, to both the front and rear of his/her car. (December)

1923

A study conducted by the Cleveland Trust Co. concluded that the "average" American car buyer was a 33-year old married male. He bought a car costing $1,400, put $700 down and paid off the balance at a rate of $100 a month. (February)

The National Safety Council declared that women were safer drivers than men. (March)

The 1924 models, promised early press releases, would include as new features both four-wheel brakes and easier-riding suspension. (June)

Henry Ford celebrated his 20th anniversary in the auto business. With a worth of $700,000,000, he was the wealthiest individual in the world. (June)

"Why Not Code Of Uniform Hand Signals For Drivers?" headlined an article in the *Sunday Telegram*. With no two states using the same set of hand signals, it was strongly suggested that it was time for some uniformity. (September)

Statistics showed that Thursday - by a wide margin - was the safest day to drive. Friday was second-safest. Sunday, especially from 3:00 PM to 8:00 PM, was the most dangerous. (November)

1924

The Cadillac Motor Car Co., with 23 dealers in Maine stretching from York to Caribou, announced it had set a Maine record by selling 241 Cadillacs in 1923. (January)

Billboards were banned in Minnesota. (January)

Maine, with 106,847 registered autos, ranked 36th in the nation. New York topped the list, with 1,002,293. (January)

The Portland Co., 58 Fore Street, Portland, advertised its High Test - "Best Motor Gasolene In Maine" - at 25¢ a gallon. (March)

Governor Percival P. Baxter bought a new V-63 Cadillac. (April)

The Forest City Filling Station in Portland installed an automobile vacuum cleaner. It was said to be especially useful "in getting all dust out of closed car upholstery." (April)

The Auto Renting Co. set up shop at 284-292 Forest Avenue, Portland. Its business: renting Ford cars or trucks by the hour, day, week or month, with or without driver. (May)

With closed cars becoming all the rage, driving was now described as "the pastime of well-dressed people." As phrased in the *Sunday Telegram*: "Milady drives to tea or Mah Jong in moire silks; the man of the family has enough confidence to trust his best suit to the family sedan." (May)

Kansas City started a campaign to remove curbside gas pumps, labeling them "unsightly" and "a public nuisance." (July)

More than 10,000 persons joined the Careful Drivers Club, formed by the Baltimore & Ohio Railroad to help reduce grade crossing accidents. Each member affixed an emblem to his/her car that read "This car stops at all railroad crossings." (December)

1925

The Franklins, with a record of 21-4, topped the Dodges to take the Auto League crown at Portland's High Street Bowling Alleys. Next came the Buicks, the Reos, and the Maxwells. (March)

John H. Mueller, Professor of Sociology at the University of Chicago, declared that the auto was breaking up home life in the United States. Said Mueller: "The automobile takes the high school and college student from the home group and makes him an enemy of society." (March)

The Franklin Journal editorialized that the owners of private cars had better wake up to the danger that the roads might soon be monopolized by trucks and busses. (May)

A new ailment, eye strain caused by staring too long at a constant stretch of white/gray road ahead, was labeled "Motorist's Eye." (May)

Dr. W.V. Bingham, Director of the Personal Research Federation in New York City, concluded that "Motor accidents are more among highly intelligent drivers than among drivers of inferior mentality." Dr. Bingham suspected this may be because the "brainy" man is more apt to have his mind "preoccupied." (September)

A *Worcester* (Mass.) *Telegram* columnist suggested, at least somewhat tongue-in-cheek, that auto dealers would do well to give cars away...as long as the recipients pledged to have all repair work done at the dealer's service center. (November)

1926

"The Sensational Automobile Comedy Drama" Six Cylinder Love - starring a 6-cylinder Hupmobile! - played the Jefferson Theatre in Portland. (February)

The auto columnist for the *Sunday Telegram* advised motorists to "keep off the roads unless absolutely necessary," stating that road conditions were so bad as to be "ruinous to any car regardless of make." (March)

Legendary long-distance swimmer Gertrude Ederle bought a brand new Reo Sport Roadster. (March)

Baseball czar Judge Kennesaw Mountain Landis came to Portland for the opening of the New England League season...and was furnished a Willys-Knight 66 sedan by Portland's Clifton Shaw, Inc. (May)

Chrysler introduced the adjustable front seat. (July)

Gabriel d'Annunzio, considered the greatest living authority on the Italian language, declared that in Italy the auto was to be considered female. "It (the automobile) has the charm, nimbleness and the liveliness of an enchantress," said d'Annunzio. (July)

Babe Ruth was voted the most popular athlete in America...and presented with an Auburn Sport Model roadster before the first game of the World Series. (October)

Hans Simonson, of Bismark, North Dakota, won a $5,000 cash prize for submitting the best name for Sears, Roebuck & Company's new tire. The name: "Allstate." (December)

1927

According to statistics published in the *Sunday Telegram*, there were 53,360 car and truck dealers in the U.S., 51,713 public garages, 83,758 gas stations and repair shops, and 66,584 auto supply stores. (January)

Pedestrians know that they are safe from the motorist driving a new car. The motorist does not care to dent his fenders the first thousand miles or so.

Portland Sunday Telegram (May)

South Dakota experimented with using a giant magnet to clean their highways. So far the magnet, seven feet wide, had hauled in a roller skate, two dozen railroad spikes, one monkey wrench, a stove leg, and "enough nails to construct a giant's castle." Officials were said to be pleased. (July)

A motorist driving through Livermore reported seeing this sign by the roadside: "Step lightly on the gas. Our Judge is a FINE man!"

Sun-up Magazine, Portland (September)

The Portland Co., 58 Fore Street, advertised High Test Gasoline for 21¢ a gallon. (September)

Judge Max L. Pinansky, Portland, characterized the practice of allowing young females to drive over Maine's roads as "unintentional suicide." Said the judge, in trying the reckless driving case of a 17-year old Portland High student: "I have a girl of my own, just about this girl's age, and she won't drive a car if I know it." (October)

1928

The "Overseas Highway," connecting Miami and Key West, Florida, was formally opened to traffic. (March)

The Henley-Kimball Co., 380 Forest Avenue, Portland, offered a 7-Days Free Trial on any and all of their used cars. (March)

Recent completion of a 200-mile stretch in Virginia brought the percentage of U.S. Route 1 (running from Fort Kent to Florida) that was hard-surfaced to 84%. (April)

The Carlton Bridge, connecting Bath and Woolwich, was dedicated. (July)

1929

Albert Russel Erskine, president of the Studebaker Corporation, stated that he believed the United States was "about to enter upon the greatest business development of its history." (January)

Several American auto manufacturers were said to be studying the possibility of front wheel drive. (March)

Jones was never an early bird at the office. One morning his boss exclaimed: "Late again. Have you ever done anything on time?"

"Yes, sir," was the meek but prompt reply. "I purchased a car."

Portland Sunday Telegram (April)

John Philip Sousa and his world famous band were heard over the radio for the first time, in an hour-long broadcast sponsored by Chevrolet to celebrate having placed over 500,000 new six-cylinder Chevys on the road in the first four months of the year. (May)

1928

Two Chicago scientists claimed, before the American Chemical Society, that they had developed a way to make motor fuel from the Douglas fir tree. (June)

Clarence C. Stetson, chairman of the Maine Development Commission, proposed a plan for more attractive filling stations and roadside stores. (October)

The stock market crashed. (October)

JOHN F. HILL CO.
WATERVILLE

John F. Hill could safely be called "Mr. Ford" around Waterville for many a year. He started out in 1917 as manager of United Garage & Sales Company, located at 24 Silver Street. Within a year he'd purchased that operation and changed the name to the John F. Hill Co. Fords were his baby, with Lincoln added in 1923. A 1923 *Waterville Morning Sentinel* article described Hill's facility as "fireproof" and with storage for 200 cars. That's a lot of cars.

John F. Hill later, in the early 1930s, switched his allegiance from Ford/Lincoln to Dodge/Plymouth. He appears to have retired from the automobile business in 1933.

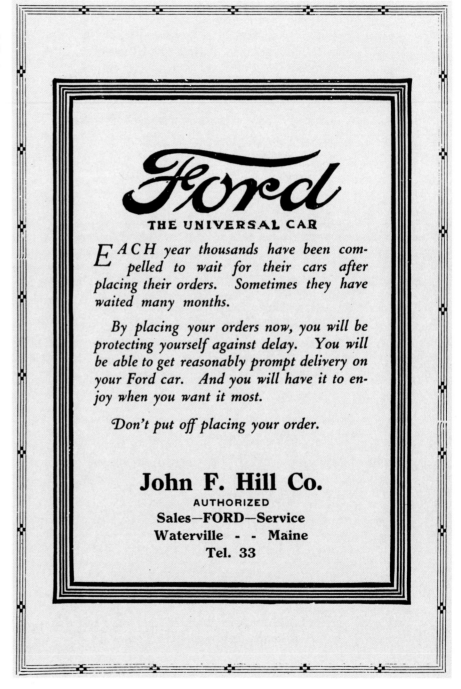

Sheet Music cover, 1928

JUST AN OLD FASHIONED AUTOMOBILE SONG

Almost from its inception the auto has been the hero of many a song. In addition to the 1928 ditty that enlivens this page, there's been *In My Merry Oldsmobile* (1905), *The Love Story Of The Packard And The Ford* (1915), and, more recently, *Little Nash Rambler, Buick '59, Hot Rod Lincoln, Pink Cadillac,* and *Gonna Find Me A Mercury* (*Mercury Blues*). Add in the many great 1950s' vocal groups that took their name from an auto marque - Bonnevilles, Cadillacs ("Speedo"), Corvairs, Corvettes, Edsels ("Rama Lama Ding Dong"), Eldorados ("At My Front Door"), Impalas ("Sorry, I Ran All The Way Home"), Lincolns, and Packards, to name a few - and you have a most impressive automobile/musical match up.

L. RAPAPORT
MILLINOCKET AND BANGOR

From Lithuania to Millinocket to Bangor. Such was the story of Louis Rapaport. Born in Lithuania, he moved to Millinocket as a youth. And it was there, in "The Magic City," that he began selling cars in 1920. He very soon expanded to Bangor as well. A 1921 ad reads "L. Rapaport, Dealer in Automobiles, Bangor/Millinocket." He sold a trio of cars not oft remembered anymore: Moon, Cleveland, and Gardner.

By 1922 Rapaport had decided to concentrate solely on Bangor. His address was 25 Salem Court. His new offerings were the Paige, and its sister car, the Jewett. Business, however, did not boom. By 1924 Rapaport, whose address by then was 118 Exchange Street, was out of the automobile business.

Louis Rapaport went on to run a meat market in Bangor. He was then longtime proprietor of the Central/New Central Furniture Company on Hammond Street. He passed away in 1966. (Ed. note: Louis' son Jack followed in his father's footsteps by operating the Rapaport Auto Company, at 32 Oak Street in Bangor, from 1946 until 1985.).

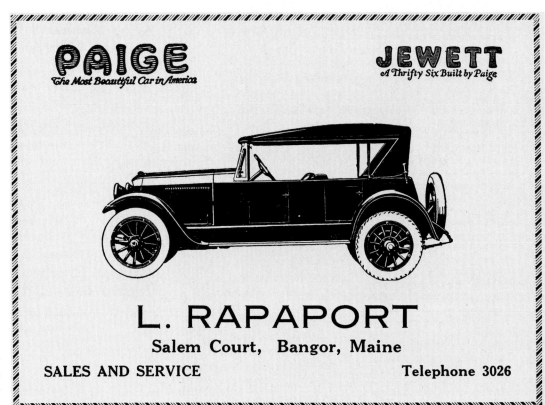

Ad, program, Bijou Theatre, Bangor, November 1922

PAIGE
The Most Beautiful Car in America

JEWETT
A Thrifty Six Built by Paige

L. RAPAPORT

Salem Court, Bangor, Maine

SALES AND SERVICE

Telephone 3026

PAIGE

The Most Beautiful Car in America

We Will Stick

Never before in the history of the Paige-Detroit Motor Car Company has there been such a demand for Paige cars. Never has the demand for Paige cars been so general. Every state, county and city of the United States is demanding a greatly increased quota. Every Paige dealer these days is active and insistent.

In our judgment these extraordinary Paige sales—in this War-Year of 1918—prove several things. They prove that the American people recognize the fact that the motor car is an indispensable utility; that they are buying motor cars carefully and intelligently; that they are buying only the best cars; that they are selecting the Paige because it is a sound, conservative, profitable war-time investment.

For this overwhelming endorsement of Paige cars, the Paige-Detroit Motor Car Company and Paige Dealers are grateful indeed. We regret that we cannot increase Paige production to satisfy every Paige purchaser and enthusiast.

Undoubtedly, you know why Paige production cannot be increased—in this War Year of 1918. We cannot discuss the tremendous expansion the Paige has made these last nine months to meet the needs of the government, the nation and the CAUSE—the greatest cause since the birth of civilization—for which it is the great PRIVILEGE of all of us to fight.

Always we will strain every nerve and energy and tax every resource to meet the needs and wishes of that vast body of sentiment that has brought us success—our Paige Patrons.

But we feel that we—and YOU—have an infinitely greater obligation to discharge, an infinitely greater task to perform. To accomplish this the Paige-Detroit Motor Car Company has pledged itself to invest every dollar of its huge capital and all the brains and braun and patriotism of the thousands of men who rally beneath the Paige Banner. We Paige men are in this Fight to Win.

"And we won't come back 'til it's over, 'over there'."

PAIGE-DETROIT MOTOR CAR COMPANY, DETROIT, MICH.

Ad, *Motor* magazine, May 1918

PAIGE

The Paige ("The Most Beautiful Car in America") and the Jewett were both products of the Paige-Detroit Motor Car Company. Located in Detroit, Paige-Detroit turned out a full line of quality cars (even ranking as the 10th largest maker of automobiles in America in 1925) from 1909 until 1928, when mounting losses caused a shutdown.

SANGERVILLE NASH SALES SANGERVILLE AND DOVER-FOXCROFT

Born in Greenville in 1861 and raised in Bradley and Pittsfield, A. (Alfonso). F. Marsh graduated from the University of Maine and lived in Old Town before settling in Sangerville as the town's druggist/confectioner in 1906. In 1921 he branched out, forming Sangerville Nash Sales, with offices in Sangerville and a showroom in Dover-Foxcroft. "It is the resolve of Nash Motors to continue to build into each Nash car such remarkable value that should it ever be impossible to get delivery on a Nash no man will accept a substitute without regret," read an A.F. Marsh ad in *The Piscataquis Observer* in August 1921

Marsh continued in the auto business, selling only Nash, until 1929. He then returned full-time to his pharmacy/candy/ice cream business until his death in the early 1940s. He is yet recalled by a select few around Sangerville. But it is for his soda fountain. "We used to think it was great to go down to the soda fountain and have ice cream sodas and one thing or another," vividly recalls Marion Race, 84. She, alas, has no recollection of Sangerville Nash at all.

Ad, program, Chadbourne American Legion Fair And Entertainment, Dover-Foxcroft, December 1922

CANAL STREET GARAGE
RUMFORD

Charles O. Dunton and William Shand repaired cars and sold Nashes at their Canal Street Garage from 1920 to mid-1925 when Shand, an Englishman who'd come to Rumford via Canada, passed away. Dunton then sold the garage to a John Sylvester. It operated, under one owner or another, through 1939.

As for Charles O. Dunton, he went on to uphold "country, family, and education" by serving as Rumford town clerk, selectman, and overseer of food for the poor. He died in Rumford, aged 77, in January 1969.

Ad, program, *The Arrival of Kitty*, senior class play, Stephens High School, Rumford, May 1923

CHARLES D. HASTY & SON
AUBURN

It was undoubtedly against Charles D. Hasty's every grain to go into the auto business. He was a horseman. Born in Raymond in 1863, Hasty took over operation of his stepfather's store in Windham upon his stepfather's death in 1879. He immediately established a livery stable in connection. In 1903 Hasty moved to Auburn, where he managed the Twitchell & Holt Company's stables at 149 Main Street. By 1905 he owned the stables. It was not until a full ten years later, in 1915, that he added the sale of autos to the sale of horses. Chevrolet was Hasty's bread and butter car, but he is known to have been agent for Velie and the Cole Aero-Eight as well.

In 1919 Hasty was joined in business by his son Bernard, back from service in the Aviation Corps. In 1921 the company name was changed to Charles D. Hasty & Son. It was to be a short union, however: Charles D. Hasty passed away in June 1922. With his dad gone, Bernard dropped the sale of horses, focusing instead on the auto side of business. He appears to have lost the Chevrolet franchise and to have moved to 155 Main Street at about the same time, in late 1929. He operated there, as a used car dealer, until his retirement in 1936.

Ad, program
U.C.T. Minstrels,
Empire Theatre,
Lewiston, March 1923

Do you believe in attractive packages? Every good merchant realizes their value.
It is equally important for a salesman to arrive at their customers
in an attractive package.

The Chevrolet Utility Coupe is an Attractive Package

CHARLES D. HASTY & SON
149 Main Street, Auburn, Maine

CHEVROLET

Cadillac, LaSalle and Marquette are autos that are/were named after French explorers. Chevrolet is an auto named after a French race car driver. His name was Louis Chevrolet. And he designed the very first Chevrolet, in 1912, for Billy Durant, founder of General Motors. Chevrolet and Durant did not see eye-to-eye, however, and Chevrolet, the driver, departed, later to resurface with the American, advertised here. As for Chevrolet, the car: well, it went on to become the largest-selling automobile in the world. (Ed note: auto dealer Louis Chevrolet, located on Center Street in Auburn, is named after Louis Chevrolet and features several impressive murals of him in its showroom.).

Ad, *Motor* magazine,
May 1918

FRED E. HALL COMPANY
HOULTON

After many years of helping out at his brother George's hay, potatoes and farm supplies salesroom, Fred E. Hall went out on his own circa 1917. And sold hay, potatoes, and farm supplies. By 1918, though, he was into autos as well, selling and servicing Buick, Dort ("Quality Goes Clear Through"), and Franklin. Fred E. Hall also sold Cadillacs for a time in 1922-21, and added GMC Trucks during that period, too. He operated on Bangor Street, until 1937.

This photo, showing one 1913 and 24 1923 Buicks, all spiffed up for the 1923 Fourth of July Parade, was undoubtedly a company highlight. *The Aroostook Pioneer* of the day rang out that "Never has Houlton had a more successful celebration." Featured was horse racing, a "Snappy Midway," "Ball Games Between Fast Teams," a "Gigantic Street Parade"...and 25 Buicks!

Photo, July 4, 1923, courtesy of Vic Thompson, Houlton

Ad, *Fortune* magazine,
May 1932

"WE'VE STANDARDIZED ON BUICKS . . . WE HAVE TWO FOR OUR FAMILY"

The new Convertible Coupe Roadster, Model 56C, $1080. The new Five-Passenger Club Sedan, Model 91, $1820. These models are typical of the twenty-six luxurious Buick body-types for 1932. All prices f. o. b. Flint, Michigan. Extremely low monthly payments on the G. M. A. C. plan.

An increasing number of families are deciding to enjoy the extra advantages of two-Buick ownership, now that Buick has the new Series 50 with eight big, luxurious models listing as low as $935 to $1155.

You, too, will find the answer to your need for an extra car among these superb new models. They are Buicks through and through. With large, roomy Bodies by Fisher, 82-horse-power Valve-in-Head Straight Eight Engine and Wizard Control, including

Automatic Clutch, Controlled Free Wheeling and Silent-Second Syncro-Mesh. And they are built with true Buick thoroughness to serve you dependably for 150,000 miles and more.

Why not call upon your Buick dealer, and learn how finely your transportation problems can be solved by the new Buick for 1932. The twenty-six models, $935 to $1155, f. o. b. Flint, Mich., provide a perfect choice for families desiring the comfort and convenience of two-car ownership.

THE NEW BUICK *with* WIZARD CONTROL

BUICK

David Dunbar Buick was a successful turn-of-the-century Michigan manu-facturer of plumbing fix-tures. Smitten with the horseless carriage, how-ever, he sold the plumb-ing business in 1899. It was to be autos for him. Unfortunately, they were unsuccessful autos. By 1903 David Buick was broke. And even though the car he developed, with improvements made to it, went on to garner fame and fortune, David Buick never really recov-ered. He died an impover-ished man at age 74 in 1929.

SPRING-DUNN MOTORS
PORTLAND

Spring-Dunn, with roots that stretched back to 1911, came into being in the summer of 1925. Co-owners were Hiram-native Fred C. Spring, in auto sales in Portland since 1908, and John M. Dunn, also an auto business veteran, who handled the financial side of the ledger. The pair, however, found themselves with a garage/showroom at 72-80 Pine Street that dated to 1914, and that was woefully inadequate for the mid-1920s. Their solution: build an addition that cost the better part of $75,000, big, big money at the time. But, as noted in the *Sunday Telegram*, the addition was "built right and exactly as the company desired it."

The firm, always exclusive Oakland/Pontiac dealers, operated until 1929 when Fred Spring left to manage a filling station, and Couri Motors (initially at 511 Forest; later 525-531 Forest) took over as agents for Oakland/Pontiac. John Dunn, doing business as Dunn Motor Company, and selling used cars, made use of the "built right" facility until 1936.

(Ed. note: When Spring-Dunn built their addition in 1925-1926 there was a city ordinance that prohibited a garage from being "too close" to a public school. With the Butler School just across Pine Street, this was a problem...solved by creating a unique curved facade that somehow kept city officialdom content. That curve yet exists today. It's well worth a look if you're ever in the vicinity of what is now labeled the 72 Pine Street/Andrews Square Building (the former Aunti Leoni's building).

Photo, May 1926, courtesy Collections of Maine Historical Society, Portland

PONTIAC

Named after the city in Michigan in which it was built (which, in turn, had been named after Chief Pontiac, noted mid-18th century leader of both the Ottawa and the Ojibwa tribes), the Pontiac was launched by General Motors at the New York Automobile Show in January 1926. Originally an off-shoot of GM's Oakland Motor Car division, Pontiac proved so popular that it eventually replaced its "parent." (Ed. note: for more on Oakland/Pontiac please see page 47.).

The facing-page photograph of a Pontiac Six sitting in front of Portland's City Hall was initially featured in the May 16, 1926 edition of the *Portland Sunday Telegram* as a part of a Pontiac publicity campaign. The idea: to guess how many miles the Six would traverse in a six-day run around Portland. The reward for closest guess: a $250.00 gift certificate good toward the purchase of any 1926 Pontiac or Oakland from Spring-Dunn.

LEON J. FORTIN
BRUNSWICK AND BATH

As with many of the dealers included in *YOU AUTO SEE MAINE*, Leon J. Fortin involved himself in several lines of work before settling in the car world. First came proprietorship of a printing operation. Then a stint with CMP's Brunswick division. By early 1924, though, he'd established Fortin's Garage adjacent to his house at 1 Mill Street. A July 1924 *Brunswick Daily Record* ad ballyhoos used cars at "Record breaking prices." Auto supplies and repairs were available as well.

Leon J. Fortin (not to be confused with his brother Victor, also a longtime Brunswick auto agent) moved into the new car end of the business by obtaining the Willys-Overland / Willys-Knight / Whippet franchise in 1927. He even branched out to Bath, operating a showroom at 55 Centre Street for a number of years. In late 1935 Fortin became agent for Dodge and Plymouth and moved to new space at 17-19 Middle Street. It was a short duration move. Leon J. Fortin took a job as machinist at BIW and retired from the automobile business in 1939. He worked at BIW the rest of his life. He died, at age 68, while eating lunch in a Bath restaurant in February 1960.

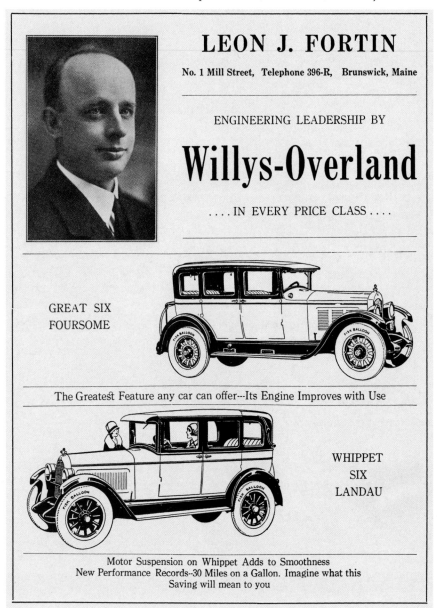

Ad, program, 50th Anniversary, St. John The Baptist Parish, Brunswick, February 1927

LEON J. FORTIN

No. 1 Mill Street, Telephone 396-R, Brunswick, Maine

ENGINEERING LEADERSHIP BY

Willys-Overland

. . . . IN EVERY PRICE CLASS . . . .

GREAT SIX FOURSOME

The Greatest Feature any car can offer---Its Engine Improves with Use

WHIPPET SIX LANDAU

Motor Suspension on Whippet Adds to Smoothness
New Performance Records--30 Miles on a Gallon. Imagine what this
Saving will mean to you

84

A Smart Practical Car for Town and Country Use

The Overland Coupe gives you all the conveniences of a limousine without the burden of a large investment.

It is comfortable and cosy on sharp, chilly March evenings; cool as an open car on hot summer days; snug and warm in real cold weather.

Any woman can drive an Overland Coupe.

The electric buttons are located on the steering column. By just pressing these buttons the car is started, stopped and lighted.

It comfortably seats four.

Deliveries can be made at once.

"Made in U. S. A."

The Willys-Overland Company
Toledo, Ohio

1915 Overland Coupe
$1600 F·O·B TOLEDO

Ad, 1915

OVERLAND

Collectively or alone, the names "Willys" and "Overland" were an important part of the U.S. car scene for over five decades. Overland first appeared in 1903. John North Willys, originally an auto dealer from Elmira, New York, arrived in 1907, taking control of the small and shaky company. Under his leadership, Willys-Overland (which also manufactured the Whippet from 1926-1931) put Toledo, Ohio on the auto-makers-of-significance map until 1954, when the concern was merged into Kaiser-Frazer. (Ed. note: Willys-Overland was instrumental in developing the Jeep, which is yet very much alive as a product of the Chrysler Corporation.).

Ad, program, U.C.T. Minstrels,
Empire Theatre, Lewiston,
March 1923

LEWISTON MOTORS
LEWISTON AND RUMFORD

Lewiston Motors could have been called Elwood P. Weeks' Motors. Weeks, a native of Jefferson, Maine, came to Lewiston in 1917, establishing E. P. Weeks & Co. at 16-18 Park Street. He sold Maxwells. In 1921 he moved next door to 20-22 Park, changed his company name to Lewiston Motors, and sold Dodge Brothers motor vehicles exclusively. In 1925 Weeks added Graham Bros. trucks to his showroom. He also sold used cars across the street, at 19-21 Park. And for a time, in and around 1928, he operated a branch in Rumford.

Ad, *Lewiston Evening Journal*,
November 5, 1927

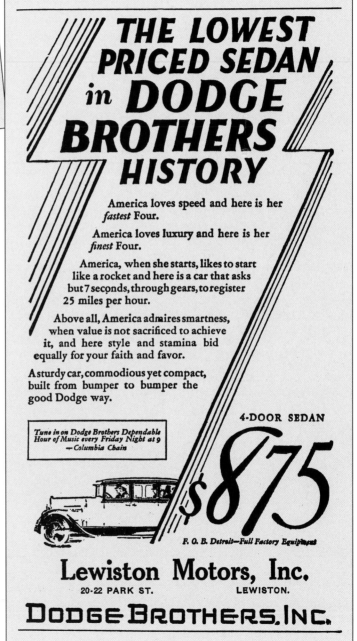

Circa 1931 Weeks appears to have lost the Dodge franchise, but he continued in operation - as a garage and used car facility - until the summer of 1934, when he closed down. Elwood Weeks was elected state senator in the fall of that same year, but had little chance to serve his constituents: he passed away, at age 56, of heart disease in January 1935.

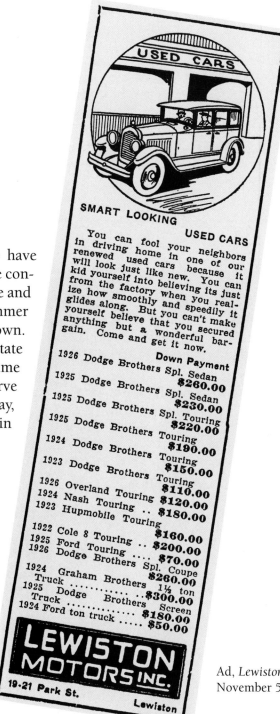

Ad, *Lewiston Daily Sun*, November 5, 1927

CLIFTON R. SHAW
LEWISTON, PORTLAND
AND AUGUSTA

Clifton R. Shaw, born and raised in Augusta, was a multiple-location pioneer. After gaining experience with his hometown Augusta Motor Company, Shaw went on his own in early 1925, establishing showrooms in Portland (365 Forest Avenue/later 517 Forest Avenue) and Augusta (corner of Cony and Bowman Streets). Both locations featured the Willys-Overland line. Lewiston (first at 48 Canal Street/later 21 Chapel Street) was added in May 1925. Whippet - a "European-type light car" - was introduced to the American motoring public - and to Clifton R. Shaw's three locations - in late 1926. In January 1928 Shaw added the Stearns-Knight. By 1930, however, Clifton R. Shaw was gone from Lewiston. His former 21 Chapel Street location was occupied by Davis Cadillac, and his former Lewiston manager, Titus Y. Springer, was set up - selling Willys and Whippets - on his own as Chapel Street Motor Sales, at 30 Chapel.

Ad, *Lewiston Evening Journal*, November 5, 1927

MORE THAN A YEAR AHEAD

1928 Features in the *Whippet* NOW !

Economy—Whippet holds A. A. A. Coast-to-Coast economy record.

Full-Vision Bodies—Whippet's narrow front pillars remove the "blind spot" hazard.

BIG 4-Wheel Brakes—Whippet is the first light car to introduce this safety feature.

THINK of the things you'd demand in a more expensive automobile for 1928—unmistakably *modern* style, attractive colors, BIG 4-wheel brakes, roominess, low center of gravity, clear-vision body, speed and lively pickup. The Whippet offers them all, plus unequaled economy of gasoline, oil and tires.

The superiority of Whippet design has been conclusively proved—in official tests and through the experience of owners who have driven their cars more than half a billion miles.

The Whippet engine is the only light car power plant which develops *twice* its rated horsepower. That is why the Whippet out-performs other cars in its price class. The advanced Whippet, in smart duotone color harmonies, is on display. Don't fail to come in and see it.

Superior Quality—New Low Prices

	Whippet	Whippet 6		Whippet	Whippet 6
Coach	$625	$795	Coupe	$625	$795
Touring	625	765	Sedan	725	875
			Landau	755	925
Roadster	695	825	Cabriolet Coupe	745	875

Prices f. o. b. factory and specifications subject to change without notice. Willys-Overland, Inc., Toledo, Ohio

CLIFTON R. SHAW, Inc.
21 Chapel St., Lewiston   Tel. 3543-W

Ad, 1927

WHIPPET

As is pointed out in the *STANDARD CATALOG OF AMERICAN CARS,* "The Whippet was wonderfully named. It was small and it was swift, and it was both those things in the superlative." Alas, however, the Whippet was not to be long-lived. A product of Willys-Overland (please see page 85), it was manufactured at the Willys' plant in Toledo from 1926 to 1931. With the Depression, Willys' management elected to cut back. The Whippet became a casualty.

PORTLAND NASH
PORTLAND
AND LEWISTON

Portland Nash joined the southern Maine auto fray in January of 1921, the brainchild of Turner native and veteran car salesman Ralph M. Bonney. The venture began life at 315 Cumberland Avenue, but was soon moved to the former home of Chandler Motors, 624-626 Forest Avenue. That location, too, proved relatively short-lived. By February 1924 Bonney and company were resettled into a building created exclusively for Portland Nash, at 353 Cumberland Avenue. It was quite the structure: 56,000 square feet spread over three fireproof floors, several showrooms, etc. "Motorist - This Nash Garage Is Some Plant" fairly shouted the company's grand opening ads, while the *Sunday Telegram* labeled the facility "one of the most completely equipped plants of its kind in this section of New England." A branch was also maintained in Lewiston. After almost a decade and a half of sales and service, Portland Nash ceased to exist in January 1935. Its operations - and its location at 353 Cumberland - were taken over by Motor Sales & Service (q. v.).

Ad, *Fortune* magazine,
May 1950

NASH

Charles W. Nash was abandoned by his parents when he was six, ran away from his court-appointed foster parents when he was 12, was head of General Motors when he was 38, and founded Nash Motors Co. in 1916 when he was 42. He founded well: Nash Motors outlived virtually all of its contemporaries, building quality cars into the 1960s and forever weaving names the likes of Ambassador, Statesman, and Metropolitan into the lexicon of the American automobile.

C.A. PINKHAM CARRIAGE CO.
FARMINGTON

"C.A. Pinkham Carriage Co." wasn't just a cute name: the company was founded by Litchfield-native C. Arthur Pinkham to manufacture carriages and sleighs. That was in the 1880s. By the early 1920s, though, C.A.'s sons, Charles J. and Robert A., saw the light and moved into autos. At first, in 1922-1923, Pinkham Carriage concentrated on auto painting. Then, in early 1924, they became an agent for Hupmobile. A 1926 ad, advertising the Hupmobile Six and Eight and showing a stern Charles and a less stern Robert, boasted "Our Plan of Action is Continued Satisfaction." Within another year the brothers added Willys-Knight and Whippet to Hupmobile. But the company's stay in the new car business was to be short. By the late 1920s the C.A. Pinkham Carriage Co. appears to have become strictly a repair/auto painting/auto parts operation. As such it remained in operation on Broadway in downtown Farmington until 1940.

RICH indeed, is the man who, with his family, can jump into the car and go—and come back happy.

The car can make or mar the trip. There is nothing more destructive of happy hours than trouble on the road with help a long and costly distance off. Just a little caution beforehand minimizes this danger to the point where you can forget it.

Bring your car in here and let us tune it for summer touring. For a very moderate charge we will completely tighten everything, lubricate every moving part by our high pressure system and put fresh oil in the engine.

We also maintain an excellent mechanical and electrical repair service station that is noted for its good work and moderate prices, and feature unexcelled automobile painting and repairing.

Prompt and Courteous Response to Help Calls

Willys-Knight Whippet Hupmobile
Authorized Sales and Service
C. A. Pinkham Carriage Co.
FARMINGTON, MAINE
C. J. PINKHAM   R. A. PINKHAM

Ad, *Sun-Up* magazine, June 1928

92

Ad, *The Horseless Age* magazine, July 13, 1910

Hupmobile

Top, gas lamps and tank, speedometer, extra.

4 CYLINDERS 20 H. P. SLIDING GEARS BOSCH MAGNETO	**$750**	(F. O. B. DETROIT) INCLUDING THREE OIL LAMPS, HORN AND TOOLS

The second year of a car that has never lost a friend—a car that continues to make good with a constantly growing list of owners that now mounts into the thousands.

HUPP MOTOR CAR CO.

Dept. E   DETROIT, MICH.

LICENSED UNDER SELDEN PATENT

HUPMOBILE

Founded by auto industry veteran Roger Craig Hupp in 1908, the Hupp Motor Car Co. rose to the big time in the 1920s, selling over 340,000 cars in the eight-year stretch between 1922 and 1929. Then along came the Depression and sales turned sour. Hupp filed for bankruptcy in 1940. It, as Hupp, Inc., continues in operation today as a manufacturer of industrial heating and air conditioning equipment.

RUSSELL'S UNDERWOOD GARAGE
YARMOUTH/FALMOUTH

Howard L. Russell was an early auto dealer in not one, but two, Maine communities. Community number one was Yarmouth, where he traded farming for auto sales and repair in 1916, forming a partnership with Sumner Leighton as Russell & Leighton at the corner of South and East Main Streets. Before two years had passed, though, Russell was on his own. And by 1921 he, now located on Myrtle Street, was a Ford agent. Next, by 1924, came Maxwell and Chevrolet. Chrysler, an outgrowth of Maxwell (please see page 25), was added in 1924/1925.

Sometime between February 1925 and February 1926 Russell moved operations to 317 Foreside Road (now also Route 88) in Falmouth Foreside. He named his place the Underwood Garage and continued to sell Chryslers. His wife Jessie ran an adjoining business that included motor camps and a filling station. In the late 1920s Russell switched makes one more time, to Hupmobile. By 1931 he appears to have bade goodbye to the auto business, although Jessie kept her side of things going to at least 1932.

**Underwood Garage   The Russells
Chrysler Sales and Service.**

Circa 1928 postcard view of the Russell's Falmouth facility, courtesy of Peter D. Bachelder, Ellsworth

Today, after many year's service as a variety /general store, the large building pictured here is home to *The Forecaster*, Falmouth, Yarmouth and Cumberland's newspaper. The structure to the left and the "Expert Crankcase Service" structure to the right have, alas, both gone the way of the Hupmobile.

Here's an ad that Howard L. Russell ran while still in Yarmouth. "Yarmouthville" was an area in Yarmouth, according to Yarmouth Historical Society director Marilyn Hinkley, that was basically in the upper village and centered around the intersection of Elm and Main Streets. It's a term that doesn't get around much anymore.

MURPHY'S GARAGE/MURPHY MOTOR COMPANY
KENNEBUNK

As suggested by the buildings pictured here (all of which still stand as Jim's Servicecenter at 21 Summer Street/Routes 35 and 9A in Kennebunk Landing: please see page 163), Murphy's Garage/Murphy Motor Company was not a gigantic operation. Longtime 1940s' next-door neighbor Lorraine Whitten comments: "They'd have two or so cars in the showroom. It was more of a gas station." (Ed. note: but the impressive line-up of vehicles included in the lower right photo, though, would certainly indicate a pretty fair volume in at least some of Murphy's earlier days.).

Andrew (Andy) Murphy opened for business in late 1927. A January 1928 ad in the *Kennebunk Star* ballyhoos the Dodge Victory Six as "The Only Car Of Its Kind In The World" and also reminds readers to "Tune in for Dodge Brothers Radio Program every Thursday night on the NBC Red Network." Murphy's sold Hudson/Essex and Graham Brothers Trucks, too. And advertised "Only Expert Mechanics Employed in Our Repair Shop."

All went seemingly well into the early 1950s when a combination of slow business and advancing age ("He was getting elderly," recalls Lorraine Whitten) caused Andy Murphy to close up shop. He retired in 1954.

All three postcard views, circa 1930, courtesy of Peter D. Bachelder, Ellsworth

PHILIP B. CROSBY
BELFAST

After both sales and service experience with a number of other Massachusetts' car dealers, Bay State native Philip B. Crosby opened his own agency, selling Willys-Knight and Overland in Springfield. That was in the early and mid-1920s. In 1927 the greener grass of Belfast, Maine called. Philip answered, opening a Dodge dealership. Plymouth was added soon thereafter, providing a one-two punch that kept Crosby's Post Office Square location humming for over four decades. In 1962 Philip B. Crosby passed away. His son, Philip B. Crosby, Jr., then took over and sold and serviced Dodge cars and trucks until business wound down in 1971. As told by Philip Crosby, Jr.: "Competition was keen. It seemed we would have one good year and then two bad." It was time to quit. The former longtime Crosby showroom is now occupied by a bank.

Ad, *The Republican Journal*, February 27, 1929

98

DODGE

John and Horace were their fist
names; Dodge their last. And in
1914-1915 they built a rather marvelous car they called Dodge
Brothers. It sold 45,000 units, a
then all-time record for a new car.
By 1920 Dodge Brothers was the
second largest auto manufacturer
in America. But it was also the year
both John and Horace died. The
company drifted for eight years,
before being purchased by Walter
Chrysler in 1928, his entrée into
the low/medium priced market.
Dodge (the "Brothers" was dropped
in the early 1930s) has been a key
factor in the success of the Chrysler
Corp. ever since.

FROST & WILKINS
BELFAST

Frost & Wilkins dated back to October 1926 when it was organized by Oscar B. Wilkins, who became its president, and Orlando E. Frost, who became its treasurer. Their salesroom was at 55 High Street and their service garage on Cross Street. They also operated a Tydol filling station in Rockland (and, later, one in Damariscotta as well.).

After experimenting with Reo and other makes, Frost & Wilkins concentrated on Studebaker. They liked to advertise: "Note! 15,000 Feet Floor Space Devoted Exclusively to the Automobile Business." The partners sold appliances and ran a very successful fuel oil business, too. Frost & Wilkins was big business.

Orlando E. Frost retired in late 1938. Oscar B. Wilkins died two years later. Oscar's widow Mabel then took over the business - with Studebaker cars and Tydol gas and fuel oil still the big guns - until 1945. Then she, too, retired, selling to a George W. Scott. Scott knew a good thing: he maintained the Frost & Wilkins' name. In fact the name lived on under the ownership of one person or another, mostly as a fuel oil distributor, until 1980.

Ad, *The Republican Journal*,
February 7, 1929

President Eight Convertible Cabriolet, for four . . . six wire wheels and trunk rack are standard equipment

*C*hampion *Eights, Proved by Time and Travel!* That precise air of smart assurance—of well-bred poise—apparent in Studebaker's champion eights, admirably demonstrates how motor cars ought to be designed. Champion speed and stamina came first, *proved* by the greatest world and international records, and by more American stock car records than all other makes of cars combined. Studebaker artists have literally interpreted this inspiring performance in coachcraft of rare grace and beauty. There is fleetness—eagerness—in every fluent line . . . and there are 78 years of Studebaker quality back of it, a matchless bulwark of reassurance.

STUDEBAKER

Builder of Champions

Ad, *Cosmopolitan* magazine, April 1930

STUDEBAKER

Beginning with electrics in 1902 (please see page 57), Studebaker rose to American automobile styling renown. Studebaker president Albert Erskine saw to that in the 1920s... and his successors saw to it right through to Studebaker's merger with Packard in 1954 and then its final ride, through 1966. All these years later who can forget Stude's "going both ways" postwar line, its sleek 1956 Golden Hawk, even its snappy 1959 Lark?

AUGUSTA OLDSMOBILE COMPANY
AUGUSTA

A native of Melrose, Massachusetts, Wesley B. Hunt began his auto sales career in Augusta in 1924 when he established The Motor Mart at 43 State Street. He sold the Maxwell/Chrysler line as well as Fisk Tires. In February 1928 Hunt lost the Chrysler franchise. His solution was to change his firm's name to the W.B. Hunt Motor Company and take on the sales/service of GMC Trucks. He also established, for a time in 1928-29, a branch in Waterville, at 10 Charles Street. Next - and last - came the Oldsmobile franchise, in early 1929, and another name change, to the Augusta Oldsmobile Company. It was to be a shortlived endeavor. Hunt was out of business by late 1932. He later managed the Taylor Shoe Company's retail outlet, the position he had when he died in Augusta, age 58, in 1956.

Ad, program, Cobbosseeconte Regatta, Augusta, July 1929

Ad, *The Horseless Age* magazine, May 28, 1902

All Roads alike to **THE OLDSMOBILE.**

$650.00 $650.00   **RUNS EVERYWHERE!**

You can pay more money for an Automobile and get more smoke, smell, noise, trouble and profanity than we can offer you. If you are anxious to experiment, don't send for our Catalog.

OLDS MOTOR WORKS,
1292 Jefferson Avenue, Detroit, Mich.

OLDSMOBILE

Having celebrated its 100th birthday in 1997, Oldsmobile certainly lives up to the first three letters of its name! Actually, auto pioneer Ransom E. Olds began building experimental cars in 1887, but it was in 1897 that he formed the Olds Motor Vehicle Co. (later Olds Motor Works) in Lansing, Michigan. Production was moved to Detroit in 1899. Ransom himself moved on to different pastures (please see page 51) in 1904. Olds became part of the fledgling General Motors in 1908 and has been a key member of the GM lineup ever since.

FOREST CITY MOTOR COMPANY
PORTLAND

Forest City, still very much in business today, has a history that stretches back a long time. The company that we know was born in 1922, but its founding proprietor, John S. Goff, had been the force behind an earlier operation that began in 1911. That operation was the Forest City Garage - agent for such now-forgotten makes as Speedwell and Velie - at 17-19 Forest Avenue. But back to 1922: Goff bought out the Peterson Motor Company, located at 327-329 Forest, changed the firm's name to Forest City, and started selling Fords and Lincolns. Goff left Forest City in 1927, and three years later, in January of 1930, Forest City dropped Ford/Lincoln and replaced them with Chevrolet. Along the way, in 1926, Forest City also changed its address, to 83 Winslow Street. Under the leadership of S. Earle Gemmer, Forest City successfully made its way through the 1930s, 1940s, and 1950s. Gemmer retired in 1957, but continued to be active in the company until his death in 1967. In 1970 Forest City moved to a 54,000 square foot facility on eight acres at 1000 Brighton Avenue. A year later the company added SAAB to its line-up. A name change was made, too, to Forest City Chevrolet/SAAB. Today, under the leadership of Todd Wenzel, Forest City is successfully making its way to the 21st century, proud of being Maine's largest volume Chevrolet dealer.

Ad, *Sun-Up* magazine, December 1929

New Ford Coupe

Being the Largest Single Ford Distributor in the State of Maine, We Carry at All Times a Complete Line of

The New Ford Pleasure Cars, Trucks and Genuine Ford Parts

Forest City Motor Co.

KILBORN B. COE, Mgr.

83 Winslow Street   Forest 6580-6581

PORTLAND, MAINE

Exclusive Lincoln Motor Car Distributors for This Territory

1933

1930

A Swedish engineer, Dr. Frederik Ljungstrom, invented an automatic transmission that was said to be practical and to work. (January)

Dodge came up with some especially "smart" names for its new car color choices. Among them: Brazil Nut Brown, Imperial Champagne, Mechanique Gray, and Flame Capucine. (January)

Mrs. James N. Downey, of the safety division of the Detroit Police Department, recommended a good breakfast as a cure-all for traffic ills. "Give a man a well-cooked breakfast and send him off with a smiling face," declared Mrs. Downey, "and half of the traffic problems will just vanish into thin air." (March)

Traffic expert W.L. Hinds, of Syracuse, New York, predicted that all major U.S. centers of population would be connected via high-speed motorways within the next 25 years. (April)

In spite of the Depression blues, auto industry heads were optimistic with respect to the future. W.S. Knudsen, head of Chevrolet, said more than 10,000 workers were to be added to the payroll, while Cadillac manager A.U. Widman expected to be re-hiring 6,000 employees. (December)

Laverne: "What was the cause of the accident at the corner today?"

Roscoe: "Two motorists after the same pedestrian."
Winthrop Winner, **magazine of Winthrop High School, Winthrop (December)**

1931

D.S. Eddins, V-P and General Manager of Oldsmobile, termed 1931 "the year of great values," projecting that "the dollar will purchase more motor car value this year than at any previous time in the history of the industry." (January)

Amelia Earhart, characterized as the "heroine of modern womanhood," signalized her fame by purchasing a Franklin Convertible Coupe. (April)

The 20,000,000th Ford arrived in Portland as part of a national promotional tour. (May)

The Bureau of Public Roads, Washington D.C., stated that toll roads were nearing extinction; that there were less than 150 miles of pay-to-ride roads remaining in the entire country. (July)

Traffic cop: "I don't care if it is Independence Day - you can't go down this street. This is a one-way street."

Dumb Dora: "Well, I'm going only one way."
Part of an ad for Battery & Service Co., Portland (July)

The Portland Co., 58 Fore Street, Portland, advertised that Tuesday, December 15th, was Dollar Day and their High Test Gasoline was 7 gallons for $1.00. (December)

1932

After driving unmolested through Cincinnati, Columbus, Philadelphia, Pittsburgh, Chicago, Washington, and New York, Norman Batzner, a Chicago salesman, was arrested in Cleveland and fined $25.00 for driving his car without license plates. "I've never had 'em," he told the judge. (January)

Car thieves in Fort Worth came up with a new twist: instead of stealing autos, the con men kidnapped them. The crooks would abscond with a car and then notify the owner where, upon receipt of their fee, the auto could be found. (May)

B.F. Goodrich introduced colored tires. Using a process called "colorweld," the tire giant implanted color pigments into the tire. Fourteen different colors and blends were available. (May)

The Waldo-Hancock Bridge, second longest suspension bridge in New England, was dedicated. (June)

A. vanDerzee, general sales manager for Dodge Brothers, issued a statement that he believed business was on the upswing. "We believe there is a definite indication that this Country is on the verge of business improvement," said the optimistic executive. (September)

Forest City Motor Co., Portland, announced a contest in which school children could earn cash prizes for submitting the best answers to the question: "Why Will Chevrolet Continue To Be A Leader in 1933?" (November)

1933

The automotive industry, stated Alon Bement, Director of the National Alliance of Art and Industry, had become the nation's foremost influence in cultivating public taste. To quote Bement: "The growing importance of beauty as a factor in modern American civilization is largely due to the cultural force of beauty in automobile design." (January)

Lewis C. Petersen was still delivering milk by horse and buggy to his patrons in Westbrook. Petersen, 83, said he was "not adverse to riding in an auto" but that he had "no inclination to drive one." (February)

Just-released statistics showed that America produced 1,094,000 cars in 1932, down from 1931's 1,897,000 and way down from 1930's 2,632,000 and 1929's record 4,249,000. The reason: the Depression. Out-of-work people don't buy new cars. (April)

The Tide Water Oil Co. promised to make its Tydol gas stations "fit in attractively with their surroundings." (April)

A General Motors executive disclosed that color preferences varied by geography. Pacific Coast buyers liked bright hues; in the southwestern states tan and gray were favored; while "maroon is much desired in the colder and more northern sections of the country, particularly in New England." (April)

America's worst road was constructed by the Packard Motor Car Co. adjacent to its plant in Detroit. It was made of granite boulders and cobblestones with holes and ruts and humps...all part of Packard's testing grounds. (October)

1934

Purely by chance, one Albert Davis, of Westbrook, was issued a Maine license plate that read AD 57. In addition to the fact that "AD" was his initials, Davis was a salesman for Heinz, famed for its 57 varieties. The coincidence landed Davis - and his plate - a photo story in the newspaper. (January)

Maine was one of 28 states that required operators of motor vehicles to be licensed. States that still did not require licensing included Texas, Oklahoma, Idaho, New Mexico, and Georgia. (March)

In what was perhaps the first car alarm, a Czech firm began installing a device which shouted "Help, Police" the moment the car was started by other than the owner. The faster the car was driven, the louder the yell. Czech police hoped this would help deter Czechoslovakia's mounting auto theft rate. (June)

A caravan of over 100 Fords departed Portland for the Chicago World's Fair. The contingent planned to reach the Windy City in four days, with a brand new Ford to be awarded to the operator of the car who made the trip "in the most economical manner." (September)

Joe: "We went to a dance last night and something happened to the taxi so we had to drive backward the whole way."

Sam: "I'll bet you didn't like that."

Joe: "Oh, I didn't mind. By the time we got there the taxi driver owed me $2.50."

Winthrop Winner, magazine of Winthrop High School, Winthrop (December)

1935

Automobile engineer Clessie L. Cummins, of Columbus, Indiana, announced plans for the introduction of a diesel motor for passenger cars. (January)

The president of the Buick Motor Car Co., Harlow H. Curtice, predicted that prosperity was on the way. Said he: "American business is on the threshold of a period of further recovery in which the advance will be more pronounced than at any time in the recent past." (February)

There were more Maine cars registered than at any time since 1931. The year-end total for 1934 was 178,995, up 10,822 from 1933. (February)

Mrs. Ruth Wallgren, of Portland, was the happy winner of a brand new DeSoto Airflow Sedan in a national "Why I Like Iced Tea" contest sponsored by the India Tea Bureau. When asked how it felt to win the Airflow, Mrs. Wallgren answered that it felt "indescribably grand." (September)

It was predicted that gasoline by the pound might be in the offing if tests conducted by the Guggenheim School of Aeronautics in New York City, where solidified gas was developed, proved viable. (November)

1936

A pair of Lubec teenagers, Eugene J. Rier and Otis McCaslin, Jr., designed and built a streamlined car with a rear engine. The auto, described by the press as "snappy looking,"sported a Chevrolet chassis with a Pontiac front end and a Willys-Knight rear end. (January)

Italians were urged to turn their cars over to the army for use in the war against Ethiopia. (January)

Nash engineers designed the new Nash and LaFayette models with the wherewithall to easily create a bed within the confines of the car. The models were now said to be "as useful at night as in the daytime." (April)

"A barber looked at a young man's sleek hair and asked him if he wanted it cut or just the oil changed."

Portland Sunday Telegram (May)

The president of the Studebaker Corporation, Paul G. Hoffman, stated that "There will always be independent auto producers in America."(November)

Henry J. Boland Co., 146 Ocean Street, South Portland, offered a free holiday turkey with the purchase of any used car in their lot. (December)

1937

New car ads were few. but there was no shortage of used car offerings. Portland's Chaplin Motor Co., 79 Preble Street, outdid the rest when it advertised 14 "As Is" cars starting as low as $39.50 (for a 1929 Plymouth coupe) and reaching only as high as $99.00 (for a 1931 Oakland sport coupe). (February)

An 11-mile stretch of highway from Romona to Julian, California was paved with gold. Really. But it was of such a low grade that it wasn't worth sending to a smelter. Officials did estimate, though, that there was a good $2,000 in value embedded in the roadway. (March)

Jenney "Solvenized" Gasoline took off in sales. Demand for the new gas jumped sales to double their normal total, stated officials of the Boston-based company. (May)

Soviet officials ordered Russian auto makers to start painting all new cars with bright colors in order to liven up the appearance of the country. Heretofore all cars had been painted black. (June)

1938

The "Typical Maine Motorist," according to a study conducted by the Maine Petroleum Industries Committee, earned from $20.00 to $30.00 a week, had never purchased a new car, and drove a second-hand car with a value of less than $200.00 (February)

Firestone, through its Auto Supply & Service Stores, introduced the pushbutton radio. (March)

Auburn inventor Dana L. McCarthy was said to be nearing completion of a device that would warn a motorist when he or she was driving too fast. The device would be set so that as soon as a car exceeded a certain speed the horn would start to blow and would continue to blow until the speed was brought below that speed. (April)

The National Traffic Safety Council announced that, of the 1,101 cities and 42 states which participated in the council's study, Memphis was the safest city in which to drive, and Massachuesetts the safest state. (May)

On the occasion of his 75th birthday, Henry Ford predicted prosperity ahead. "We" he said, "will keep right on going forward, discovering methods of increasing manufacture, improving production and inventing things to make things better for people." (July)

Inmates at Southern Michigan State Prison who were up for release were given special traffic safety instructions before being allowed to again venture forth on the streets and highways. (November)

1939

Selling cars is as easy as 1-2-3, stated Buffalo, New York auto salesman par excellence Harvey Stowers. People with square jaws, such as Jack Dempsey and Mussolini, value strength. Sell them on the strength and durability of a car. A person with a triangular head is a romantic. Sell them on beauty. And a fat man or woman is interested in comfort. "That's," summed up Stowers, "what made him or her fat." (February)

In an attempt to spur sales, Oldsmobile gave away a new Olds Sixty every day for 31 straight days. All a person had to do to have his/her name entered in the contest was to "visit your neighborhood Olds dealer and fill out an Official Entry Blank."(February)

Maine's first drive-in, the Saco Open Air Auto Theatre (now the Saco Drive-In), opened for business. (July)

1935

A Gallup Poll showed that Americans - by a wide margin - felt safer riding with a male driver than a female. Fully 60% were in favor of a male, vs. but 8% in favor of a female. The remaining 32% said that had no preference. (July)

The Atlantic Coast Line Railroad advertised its Ship-Your-Car plan, whereby you could send your car to Florida by rail as long as you were paying to go by rail yourself. (December)

Ad, program, Wesserunsett Valley Fair, Athens, September 1930. (You have to get a chuckle out of how they spelled "Motor.").

MADISON MOTOR CO.
MADISON

"He was one of those men who didn't gyp you when you traded with him." So recalls 93-year old Dorothy Billings Counts in discussing Everett Sawyer, the man behind Madison Motors. Sawyer opened for business circa 1925 in a structure that was being used by a local Ford dealer, Holt & Hight. Sawyer had worked for H & H; then bought them out and commenced his own operation. Ford and Chrysler were handled at one time or another. Dorothy Billings Counts remembers Sawyer would have two cars on display on the first floor of his two-floor building at 48 Main Street. "It was not," she laughs, "a big showroom." Madison Motors operated all through the lean Depression years. In 1940, though, Everett Sawyer closed down. Reflected *The Madison Bulletin* in a February 1, 1940 article: "It is not known what will be done with the building." (Ed. note: the former showroom/garage still stands, occupied by the Madison-Anson Community Federal Credit Union.).

Cars   Trucks

FORD

AUTHORIZED SALES AND

SERVICE

—o—

Madison Moter Co.

Madison, Maine

Phone 113   Farmers' 9-13

FORD

When Henry Ford built his first auto in a shed behind his house in Detroit in the summer of 1896, he had to knock down one of the shed's walls to get his creation out: he'd neglected to realize that the shed's door was too small. It was, perhaps, one of the very few mistakes that Henry Ford made in his long life. When he died at the age of 83 in 1947, *Life* magazine wrote "The Father of the Automobile Dies." While some might disagree with "The Father" part of that statement, few would not acknowledge that Mr. Ford did more to revolutionize the automobile industry than any other single human being past or present.

UTTERBACK-GLEASON CO.
BANGOR

Utterback-Gleason was the union of John G. Utterback, one-time mayor of Bangor, and James I. Gleason. They teamed up in 1914 and sold, through the years, Dort, National, Kissel Kar, Maxwell, Chrysler, and Plymouth. For most of its early years in the auto business Utterback-Gleason was located at 142 Exchange, with a move to 281 Main in 1926 and a last move to 15 Oak Street in 1936. Auto sales ceased in 1942, but a separate operation at 44 Broad Street that sold appliances, paint, and leather goods was operated until the late 1970s.

MURRAY MOTORS
BANGOR

Murray Motors was a spinoff of Charles Murray's Murray Motor Mart, which was in business from 1931 until 1975, and which was advertised in its early years as "Maine's Most Modern Garage." Murray Motors was much shorter lived, selling Dodge, Studebaker, Rockne, Pierce-Arrow and Plymouth at its 110-122 Franklin Street location from 1932 to 1937.

DARLING AUTOMOBILE CO.
BANGOR

For information on Darling please see page 50.

Ad, program, Bangor Auto Show, Bangor, March, 1935

112

PLYMOUTH

Plymouth - named to reflect the strength and endurance of the Pilgrims - was Walter Chrysler's entry into the low-priced field, his answer to Ford and Chevrolet. The timing couldn't have been much better. Launched with great fanfare in 1928, Plymouth was a major factor in seeing the Chrysler Corp. through the Depression. And it's been a top seller ever since.

INVEST IN "THE CAR THAT STANDS UP BEST"

8 **The Big 1938 Plymouth De Luxe 4-Door Sedan with trunk** delivers in Detroit for $815—other models as low as $645—including Federal taxes. State, local taxes not included. See a Dodge, De Soto or Chrysler dealer—*today!* PLYMOUTH DIVISION OF CHRYSLER CORPORATION, Detroit, Michigan.

TUNE IN MAJOR BOWES' ORIGINAL AMATEUR HOUR — COLUMBIA NETWORK, THURSDAYS, 9 TO 10 P. M., E.S.T.

Ad, *Fortune* magazine, April 1938

RIPLEY & FLETCHER CO. SOUTH PARIS AND BRIDGTON

With a birthdate of 1908, Ripley & Fletcher is the oldest still-in-business auto dealership in Maine. The "Ripley" was Perley F. Ripley, who was born in West Paris in 1875 and who had considerable retail experience working in the village store in Paris Hill. The "Fletcher" was Herbert G. Fletcher, a longstanding barber in South Paris. The pair pooled their savings and their creativity and incorporated all those many years ago, when both the automobile and the 20th Century were young.

Fords were sold almost from the beginning. The very first sale of one was to George M. Atwood, owner and publisher of *The Oxford Democrat*, in early 1910. A total of ten Fords were sold in 1910. In the years just before World War I Dodge was also sold; ditto for Cadillac in the early 1920s. But mostly it was Fords (and Lincolns). Ripley & Fletcher has sold a lot of them. There's an old saying around South Paris, in fact, that goes: "To be recognized

Ad, *The Bridgton News*,
May 24, 1935

as a select person one had to belong to the Congregational Church, have one's hair cut at Pokey French's, and buy one's car at Ripley & Fletcher." For some years Perley Ripley was involved in three dealerships. There was Cook-Ripley (later Ripley Motors, q.v.) in Portland, Ripley & Fletcher in Bridgton (which operated from 1919 to 1941) and, of course, the flagship operation in South Paris.

Perley F. Ripley was also president of the local Paris Trust Co., the first president of the Maine Automobile Dealers' Association, and (in the 1930s and early 1940s) owner of the Falmouth Hotel in Portland. He died of heart failure in August 1945.

There are today no Ripleys or Fletchers involved in Ripley & Fletcher. But the name lives on. So does the sale of Fords. Ripley & Fletcher can claim to be the oldest continuously-in-operation Ford dealership in New England. I asked Grant Jones, present-day R & F general manager, if he felt like a part of history. His reply: "A little bit. It's an old establishment. Once in a while you think about that stuff." (Ed. note: Ripley & Fletcher is in the same building they've been in since 1912 or so, but it has been remodeled to such an extent you'd never know it.).

Ad, *The Eureka*, magazine of Woodstock High School, Bryant Pond, Spring 1922

RIPLEY MOTORS PORTLAND

Perley F. Ripley sold a lot of Fords and Lincolns. Born in West Paris in 1875, he joined forces with Herbert G. Fletcher to form Ripley and Fletcher (q. v.) in South Paris (and later Bridgton) in 1908. It's Perley Ripley's Portland operation, however, that interests us here. That began in January 1929, when Ripley and Arthur P. Cook purchased the Portland Auto Sales Company, changing the name to Cook-Ripley, and changing location to a brand-new facility at 530 Forest Avenue. The Cook/Ripley partnership, though, was to be a relatively shortlived one. By December 1933 Cook was gone, and the firm's name changed to Ripley Motors.

In January 1935 Ripley added a former All-American tackle named Jim Tanguay to his sales staff. "If he (Tanguay) bucks the lines of sales resistance and gives the same type of interference for the snappy Ford car as he has in football, there will be many touchdowns this year for Ripley Motors," ran a "puff" article in the January 13, 1935 *Portland Sunday Telegram*.

By 1941 Perley Ripley, at age 66, was undoubtedly feeling spread thin. He sold his Portland business to Champion Motors, the better to concentrate on his South Paris base.

Ad, *Portland Press Herald*, May 6, 1937

(Ed. note: Rowe Motors, included here as a sub-dealer, is yet very much in operation in Westbrook. Founded by South Portland-native Raymond B. Rowe in 1920 as Westbrook Garage and Machine Co., it can today bill itself as "One Of Ford's Top Volume Dealers In New England.").

LINCOLN

The Lincoln Motor Co. was actually organized to produce aircraft engines during World War I. But the war ended before the firm's military effort could get under way. Management (which included Henry Leland, the "father" of the Cadillac) solved that problem by turning to the luxury car field. Production problems, though, set in early and by early 1922 Lincoln was in receivership. In stepped Henry Ford, who knew a good thing: he purchased the company and all its assets for $8,000,000. The Lincoln has been Ford's top-of-the-line automobile all these years since.

Ad, *The Saturday Evening Post*, October 12, 1940

MOTOR SALES & SERVICE
PORTLAND

Motor Sales & Service took over the former Portland Nash (q.v.) operation in January of 1935. Headed by Ralph M. Bonney, the Turner native/Bates College grad who'd headed up Portland Nash, the firm continued to sell and service Nash, as well as Nash's sister car, the LaFayette. Bonney brought the line-up to three with the addition, almost immediately, of Packard. It was to be short-lived. Nash and LaFayette were dropped by early 1936. Bonney went it alone with Packard until he took on Studebaker, too, in late 1939.

In the beginning, Motor Sales & Service operated at 353 Cumberland Avenue. It moved, in July 1935, to 495 Forest Avenue. Its last move, in 1937, was to 517 Forest.

In April 1942 Ralph Bonney merged his operation into Champion Motors, up the avenue at 530 Forest. Motor Sales & Service was no more.

(Ed. note: the ad's "NO state sales tax" words were true. West Virginia was the first state to place a tax on sales, in 1921. Maine didn't so tax its citizenry until 1951.).

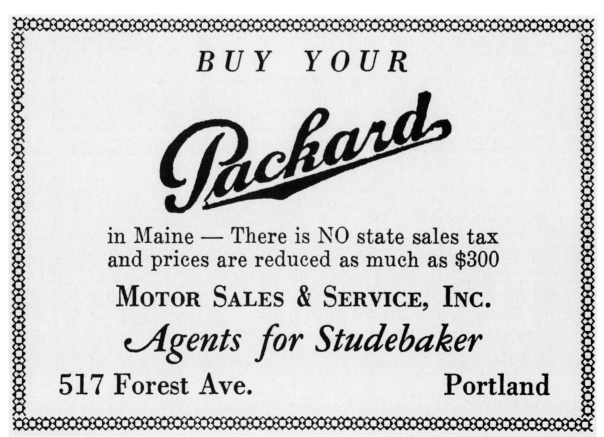

BUY YOUR

Packard

in Maine — There is NO state sales tax and prices are reduced as much as $300

MOTOR SALES & SERVICE, INC.

Agents for Studebaker

517 Forest Ave.   Portland

Ad, *High Tide magazine*, July 13, 1940

118

PACKARD

That automobile legend, the Packard, took its name from its maker: James Ward Packard. The story goes that Mr. Packard bought a Winton (q. v.) in 1898, was dissatisfied with it, complained, and was told by Mr. Winton that if he (Mr. Packard) thought he could build a better car then he should go ahead and build it. The rest, as they say, is history: sixty years - 1899-1958 - of marvelous Packard motor cars squarely attest to that.

Ad. *Portland Press Herald,* October 6, 1937

MARDEN MOTOR CO. AUGUSTA

Edgar S. Marden certainly qualified as one of Maine's most enduring car dealers. After a stint in the Army during World War I, the Vassalboro native came to Augusta and jumped on the auto bandwagon as manager of Waterville Motor Company's Augusta operation, located at 4-8 Bangor Street. Waterville Motors sold Studebakers ...and so would Marden the remainder of his long career.

In late 1926 the Portland-based Hennings Motor Company, also a Studebaker dealer, took over at 4-8 Bangor. Marden stayed on as manager. In March 1928 he made his move: he bought Henning's Augusta operation and became the Marden Motor Company. He celebrated with an exhibition of Studebakers in May that he touted, in ads in the *Kennebec Journal*, as "the most comprehensive showing of these champion cars ever made in this city."

Studebaker Commander
the car that sells itself in a 10-mile demonstration

MARDEN MOTOR CO.
314 STATE STREET   AUGUSTA, MAINE

No other car, regardless of price, gives you all these Studebaker features at no extra cost

- **Planar independent suspension**
  . . . **The famous Miracle Ride**
- **Automatic hill holder**
  No rolling back on up-grade stops
- **Non-slam rotary door latches**
  . . . **Finger-touch closing**
- **One-piece steel body reinforced by box section steel girders**
  . . . **Battleship construction**
- **Fram oil cleaner and floating oil screen**
  . . **Better oil and motor economy**
- **Finest hydraulic shock absorbers**
  . . . **Lullaby comfort**

- **Variable ratio steering**
  Easier parking and better control
- **Horizontal transmission**
  . . . **Restfully level front floors**
- **Oversize weather-tight trunk**
  . . . **Giant luggage capacity**
- **Front seat 55 inches wide**
  . . . **Seats three comfortably**
- **Safety glass all around**
  . . . **Indispensable protection**
- **Feather-touch hydraulic brakes**
  . . . **Swift, sure stopping**
- **Hypoid gear rear axle**
  . . . **Greater quiet**

Front and rear bumpers, bumper guards, metal spring covers, two windshield wipers, fender tail lamp, license bracket tail lamp, sun visor, cloth upholstery, five painted disc wheels, extra tire and tube. Vacuum-actuated Miracle Shift and Gas-saving Automatic Overdrive available at extra cost.

In 1930 Marden added Pierce-Arrow to his line. Rockne, a Studebaker product named in honor of fabled Notre Dame coach Knute Rockne, came on board in 1932. But it was Studebaker that was the love of Edgar Marden's business life... a business life that saw him move to larger quarters at 314 State Street in 1934 and saw him hang in there during Studebaker's dog days in the mid and late 1950s. Finally, in 1960, Edgar S. Marden sold the business and retired. He passed away in Augusta, at age 86, in October 1978.

Ad, *Fortune* magazine, April 1938

PONTIAC 39 SIX

Two Door Trunk Sedan. Metallic Grey. Heater, Defroster. Excellent. **$595**

1940

1940

Owen Moore's store in Portland advertised television for the very first time in Maine. In-store demonstrations were on tap both Monday and Tuesday, February 19th and 20th. (February)

The *Sunday Telegram* made a case for 94-year old Walter A. Gowen, of Biddeford, as the nation's oldest driver. The paper wrote that Gowen, a Civil War veteran and retired Boston & Maine engineer, " handles his machine through the heavy traffic with fully as much skill as he engineered many of the crack express trains of the Boston & Maine." (May)

Henry Ford and his team of mass production experts announced they were set to study the Curtiss P-40 with an eye toward turning out a 1,000 planes a day if the need arose. (June)

All the major auto manufacturers began to retool and to ready themselves for a possible war effort. Chrysler erected a $20,000,000 plant for the production of tanks. Packard was set to roll with airplane engines. Ditto Ford, while GM suddenly found itself in the machine gun business.

"Brighter colors and new, crisp patterns" marked the upholstery fabrics chosen by auto makers for their 1941 models. The result was said to be, more than ever, "a living room on wheels." (October)

"Isn't it wonderful," said Matilda, "how those service stations dig down and find gas every time."
The Oracle, magazine of Bangor High School, Bangor (October)

Clyde G. Abernathy, of Hornell, New York, developed a technique whereby, he claimed, roads, airports and bridges could be made to be invisible. It was thought his technique would be invaluable in thwarting possible enemy air attacks. (December)

1941

Despite the threat of war the auto industry announced that 1941 would be a big year for car production. (March)

Maine's first draftees, stationed at Fort Bragg, North Carolina, reported they found the climate, the grits-and-gravy for breakfast, and the "you all's" strange and difficult to get used to. (May)

"Gasless Sundays" cropped up from Maine to Florida as the East Coast wrestled with a dwindling supply of gasoline. Most stations in Maine raised their price a 1/2¢ a gallon, from 18 1/2¢ to 19¢. (August)

In a "Buy Wisely - Buy Plymouth" ad there was included a listing of the "Products Of Chrysler Corporation." Passenger cars came in fifth, after army trucks, anti-aircraft guns, aircraft parts, and army vehicles. (September)

Instead of horses, cattle rustlers used trucks. In Utah, especially, it was reported that "Large trucks roaming country roads in bright moonlight have picked up cows and calves and vanished with them." (November)

The Japanese bombed Pearl Harbor and FDR and Congress declared war. (December)

1942

With few new cars in the offing, Buick dealers throughout Maine talked up the need for a thorough spring conditioning. "A lick and a promise won't do this year, mister," ran ad copy, adding "You've got a whole car that will have to see you through the duration."(February)

Joseph W. Frazer, president of Willys-Overland, suggested that America's 40,000 car dealers turn their shops into miniature war arsenals... "by using their grinders, lathes, drill presses and other machine tools for light manufacturing to aid the war effort."(March)

President Roosevelt urged that a nationwide top speed of 40 miles per hour be put into effect in order to conserve rubber. "Rubber experts agree," stated the president, "that fast driving wastes rubber and that tires run many more miles when driven at limited rates of speed." (March)

Tokio, Arkansas decided, after much debate, not to change its name.

Cutbacks in autos, tires, and gas led to more bicycles. Ownership of the two-wheelers was up over a 1,000,000 from 1940. (May)

Mainers turned in over 111 tons of scrap rubber to service stations, which served as collection points throughout the state (June), while 192,000 cars were scrapped in the six New England states, providing enough metal for 240,000,000 hand grenades. (December)

William B. Stout, designer of an experimental car called the Scarab, wrote in the *MIT Review* that the motor car would enjoy a "glorious revival" when peace returned... that "waste will be eliminated: we will swing away from the decorative to the functional." (December)

1943

Maine was second in the nation in the national scrap drive. Maine was at 113.9% of its quota. Only New Jersey, with 115.8%, was higher. (January)

Charles W. Nash, founder of Nash Motors Co., predicted postwar cars would be "lighter, smaller, and cheaper." (April)

The fireflies at night were so dense in the Rockland/Rockport area that Civil Defense forces mistook them for saboteurs signaling to submarines. (June)

Maine's governor, Sumner Sewall, urged every eligible female not employed in the war effort to join the WACs. (Women's Army Corps) (September)

Gen. Dwight D. Eisenhower, broadcasting from Algiers, warned that an Allied victory was a "long, long way off." (October)

1944

"For Moral's Sake Be Lovely At All Times," advertised the Beverly Beauty Salon, Chapman Arcade, Portland, in ballyhooing its "Individualized Oil Permanent." (February)

Chevrolet ads featured Chevy's Six Star Service Special... to "make your car run better - last longer - serve for the duration." (February)

Taxi service in Keene, New Hampshire was resumed after a four-day shutdown due to lack of gas. (March)

Ford's Willow Run (Michigan) plant produced its 5,000th B-24 Liberator bomber. (June)

The Department of the Interior announced it had set up an Office of Synthetic Liquid Fuels to undertake the development of gas and oil from sources other than natural petroleum. (October)

1945

Peace rumors swept Boston, with newspaper offices and the police department deluged with calls hoping to verify that Germany had surrendered. (March)

FDR died at the "Little White House" in Warm Springs, Georgia. (April)

Germany surrendered! (May)

It was announced that Maine shipyards had produced an amazing 1,358 war-effort ships since Pearl Harbor. (June)

Japan surrendered! (September)

Champion Motors, 530 Forest Avenue, Portland, announced that the new 1946 Ford - "the most beautiful Ford ever built"- was on display in its showroom. (October)

Henry Ford, 82, retired as head of the company he founded in order to pursue "other interests." (December)

1946

Kaiser, "the first American car in the low priced field to have front wheel drive," was introduced to the American motoring public. (January)

Strikes and material shortages combined to keep new-car production well below initial estimates. (March)

The first Crosley - an all-economy car that weighed less than 1,150 pounds - rolled off the Crosley assembly line at Marion, Indiana. (May)

Display models of the streamlined 1947 Studebaker - characterized as "The First Postwar Designed Auto" - arrived in Maine. (June)

Waiting lists were the norm for prospective new car buyers. A Buick ad - "What Other Car Has So Much That Clicks For Forty-Six?" - said it all: "The great Buick factories are turning them out as fast as they can get materials. So put your name on our list and get one headed your way."(September)

George Romney, general manager of the Automobile Manufacturers' Association, estimated that the year's coal and steel strikes would cost the automotive industry 1,200,000 cars and trucks in 1946. (November)

1947

The James Bailey Co. (remember them: see page 18) celebrated its 101st birthday by slashing prices on selected sporting apparel by 50%. (January)

Henry Ford died at age 83, ending what was termed "one of the most romantic careers in American industrial history." (April)

It was announced by Dr. Henry Hinton, professor of chemistry at Notre Dame, that a synthetic/non-petroleum oil that would last the lifetime of a car without having to be changed was about to go into production. (April)

Traveling at speeds that sometimes surpassed 60 miles per hour, president Harry S Truman "chauffeured" himself from Charlottesville, Va. to the White House in a Cadillac convertible...with the top down. (July)

A squadron of flying saucers was reported "zipping" over Augusta. (July)

It was stated that the automotive industry was as much as a year behind in filling new car orders. Things were so bad that, it was further stated, dealers were discouraging new car buyers or flatly refusing to take additional orders. (August)

1948

The auto industry's backlog of unfilled orders was estimated to be at 6,000,000. (January)

The dealers along Auto Row in Portland held their first Washington's Birthday Open House in seven years. (February)

Hudson heralded its 1948 models as "the only car you step *down* into," giving Hudson "unique beauty not possible in any other type of car." (April)

Buick advertised its new Dynaflow Drive as "Sheer Travel Magic," allowing drivers to "glide over ground and grades in swift and utter smoothness as constant and unbroken as Niagara's flow." (July)

A federal House of Representative's probe discovered that it was of little use for a prospective new car buyer to put his/her name on a waiting list; that what new cars there were seemed to be going to customers who gave the salesman a tip or were willing to let their trade-in go cheap. (November)

A *Lewiston Evening Journal* help-wanted ad offered a chance to earn as much as $10,000 a year being an auto salesman for one of the big three manufacturers. (December)

1949

Henry J. Kaiser blasted the Federal Reserve Board's limitations on installment buying, saying that he was cutting his auto output from 675 cars a day to about 400 "or maybe less." He said the Board's credit restrictions were the cause. (January)

Twenty-four well-chosen words made Kenneth H. Roderick of South Portland $1,000 richer and the owner of a 1949 Kaiser Traveler. In a national "Why I Like the Kaiser" contest, Roderick penned "It gives roomy comfort, easy driving, and leads in design of a large car at the cost and gas economy of a small one." It was good enough to earn him the $1,000, good toward the purchase of any Kaiser. (May)

1947

A Denver, Colorado auto dealer proclaimed his One-Cent Sale a huge success. Here's how it worked: a customer bought either a new Hudson or a top-of-the-line used car...and could then select a lower-priced used car for a penny. (May)

"For goodness sake, use both hands!" smiled Lois in the car.

"I can't," said Carl. "I have to steer with one."
> **The AQUILO, yearbook of Ricker Classical Institute, Houlton (June)**

The nine-passenger Royal station wagon, Chrysler's first station wagon since 1941, was introduced to the public by Maine's Chrysler dealers. (October)

"Roses are red, violets are blue,
Sugar is sweet, but we tell you true,
The sweetest thing in the new-car line
Is the Studebaker for 'forty-nine!'"
> ad, Marden Motor Co., Augusta (December)

BROADWAY AUTO SALES
SOUTH PORTLAND

With few exceptions, YOU AUTO SEE MAINE is the story of past and present *new* car dealers. This is one of those exceptions. I just liked the photo on the facing page a lot.

Broadway Auto Sales, seller of used cars only, opened for business in 1940. Its location was 585 Broadway, diagonally across from what was then South Portland High and is now the Mahoney Middle School. Proprietors were Henry Martin and Roger Converse. Within a year Martin was gone and Converse was sole proprietor. Early ads, during those auto-shortage war years, promised "Highest Cash Prices For Good Used Cars."

Roger Converse ran Broadway Auto Sales through all of the 1940s. In 1949, he moved his residence to Camden. It was a tough commute to South Portland. He sold the business in 1950. The building that housed Broadway Auto Sales continued on as a gas station, the South Portland Filling Station, through 1996. It's today the home of Pine Tree Quilt Works.

Ad, *Portland Sunday Telegram*, September 6, 1942

We'll Buy Your Car
Regardless of Year
★ ★ ★ ★ ★ ★ ★ ★
Duration Transportation
1939 BUICK
SPECIAL SEDAN
Radio and Heater. Exceptional condition.
Many Others To Choose From.
Broadway Auto Sales
585 Broadway   4-2831   So. Portland
(Opp. So. Portland High School)

"Duration Transportation" translated to "It's no creampuff but it'll make it through the War."

Photo, May 1948, courtesy of Sullivan Photo, Portland

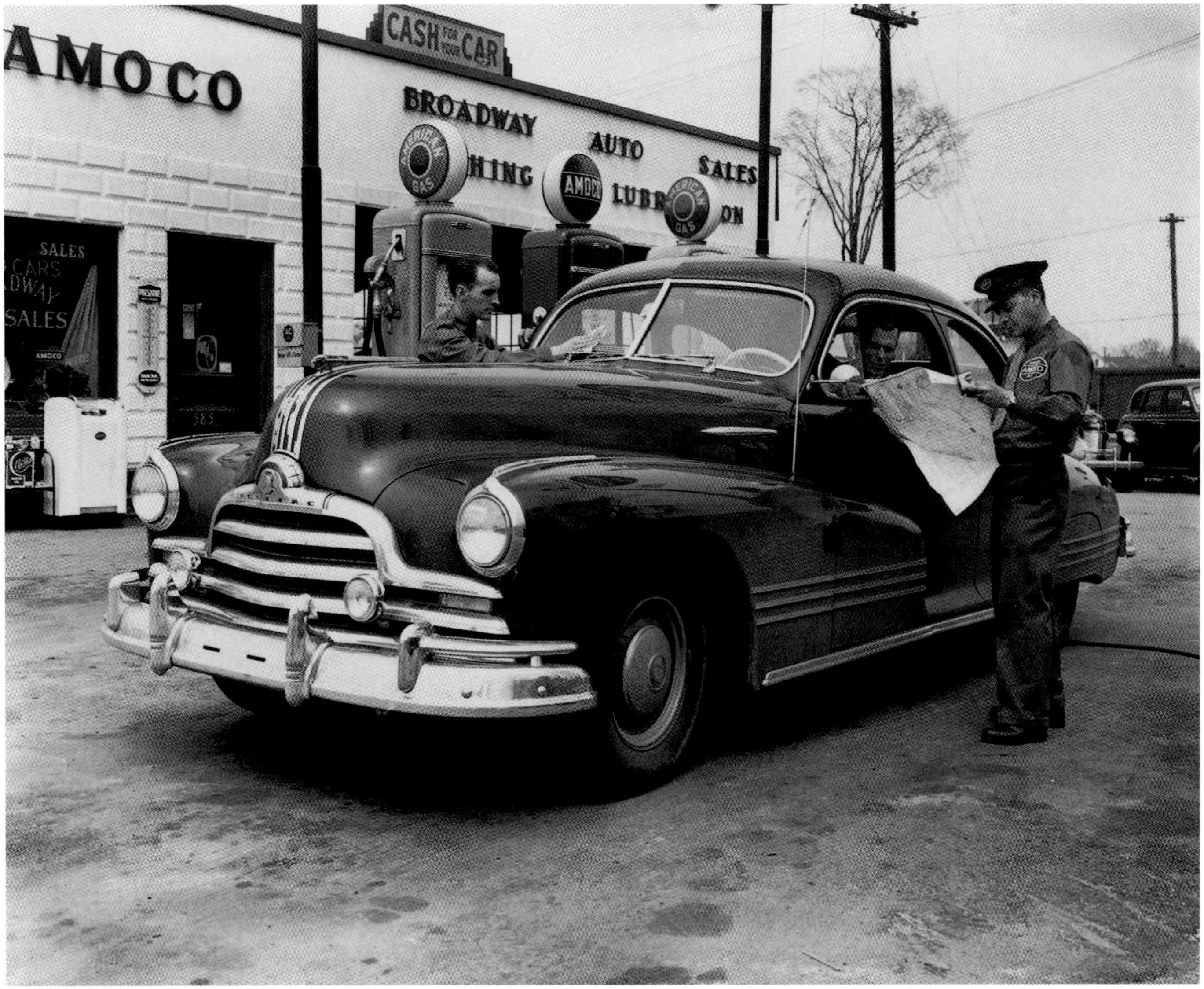

GRAND TRUNK GARAGE
PORTLAND

The Grand Trunk Garage, located off the automobile showroom beaten path on India Street, began with used cars and ended with used cars. In between, though, came a flirtation with Kaiser-Frazer. It all started in 1929 when Russian immigrant Max Astor, then 33, decided to go out of the clothing business and into the auto business. At first it was just "Max Astor, Auto Repairs," at 73-75 India, but in 1932 Max formalized to the Grand Trunk Garage (named after the nearby Grand Trunk Railway depot) and began to sell used cars as well as repair them. A 1935 ad offers "100 Cars To Choose From," and prices that ranged from $25.00 on up to $400.00.

The big excitement, though, came in 1945 when Grand Trunk took on the sale of Kaiser-Frazer, hailed in Grand Trunk ads as the only cars with "total postwar engineering and styling." Max expanded across the street to 60-66 India and also stocked rototillers and a "complete line of farm equipment." With promotions that rang "This is not a bank, but we save you money," Grand Trunk did its best for Kaiser-Frazer. They eventually parted company, however, with the K-F franchise moving to newly-formed Kaiser-Frazer Sales, 53 Winslow Street, in March 1951. It was then back to used cars exclusively for Grand Trunk. In 1964 the name of the business was changed to Astor Motor Co. It

remained in operation, at 60 India only, until 1968 when the building was demolished and Max Astor retired to Florida. He passed away in April 1989, aged 92.

(Ed. note: Max Astor's son, Dave, who worked at Grand Trunk as a salesman/sales manager, was *the* Dave Astor who hosted "For Teenagers Only" on Portland television from 1956 to 1971. For many of those years Grand Trunk, not surprisingly, was a sponsor.).

Ad, *Portland Sunday Telegram,* June 8, 1947

WE WANT YOUR CAR

"THIS IS NOT A BANK BUT YOU SAVE MONEY"
WE'LL PAY A LOT MORE THAN YOUR CAR IS WORTH
THE PLACE
KAISER-FRAZER
TRADING POST

THIS WEEK'S SPECIAL
1939 CHEVROLET MASTER DE LUXE SEDAN $525

Twenty-Seven More To Choose From At Greatly REDUCED PRICES
ALWAYS OUT FRONT WITH THE BEST
PORTLAND'S LIVE WIRE DEALER
WHO SAYS — COME EARLY! SEE! SAVE!
IT'S GRAND TRUNK GARAGE, PORTLAND
73 INDIA ST.   DIAL 3-4793
TO SELL OR BUY — LET'S MEET — WE'LL TRY

Production schedules **doubled** at Willow Run this year!

Compare the Ride!

KAISER and FRAZER owners say they enjoy a *ride* unequaled in any other car. Try it!

The Frazer Manhattan!

In nine months it has become the largest-selling car in its class! Because it offers buyers the greatest postwar *value!*

LAST YEAR, we produced 125,000 KAISER and FRAZER cars. While this broke all production records for a first year in the industry, it was only the beginning. For we still have tens of thousands of waiting customers.

This year we will do far better. The world's only 100% postwar automobile plant is about to hit its full stride! Willow Run has the capacity—and we have scheduled production at a rate *double* that of 1947. So go to your nearby K-F dealer and discover the difference between *prewar* and *postwar* cars! *Drive* one of these sensational products of ultra-modern engineering and styling! You can get one, now, almost as soon as you would like to have it.

KAISER·FRAZER CORPORATION • WILLOW RUN, MICHIGAN

KAISER-FRAZER

Kaiser-Frazer was formed in 1945, the union of shipbuilder extraordinaire Henry J. Kaiser and longtime auto man Joseph W. Frazer. The sky was to be their limit. But, after a most successful 1947 and 1948, the duo ran into GM, Chrysler, and Ford. The "Big Three" proved too much for K-F. The years 1949 and 1950 were bad ones. After an upswing in 1951, sales continued to drop steadily down. The end result, in 1955, was the halt of all production.

Ad, *Collier's* magazine, December 6, 1947

PORTLAND BUICK COMPANY
PORTLAND

Portland Buick appeared on the scene in mid-1923, managed by Carl L. Curtis, a Farmington native who also headed up the Lewiston Buick Company. Portland Buick's first location was 642 Congress Street, but by September of its initial year the company had a showroom and service center in operation at 59-69 Preble Street. The operative word here may well have been "service." Perhaps more than any of its contemporaries, Portland Buick stressed service and maintenance: a December 1933 *Sunday Telegram* article heralded the company's new Specialized Lubrication department, and went on to state the "The Portland Buick Company has the belief that the most complimentary thing that a motorist can say about a dealer is 'They give wonderful service."

In 1941 - just a year before the photo included here was taken - Portland Buick moved down Preble to larger space at 73-85. Not much else of great consequence happened until 1956 when C. William Fogg, who'd owned Portland Buick since 1951, retired to Florida, selling the company to John C. Haverty. The sale meant the end of Portland Buick. Haverty promptly changed the name to Haverty Buick. (Ed. note: when in Portland drive up Preble Street to see how little changed Portland Buick's old building is.).

Photo, July 1942, courtesy of Sullivan Photo, Portland

Circa 1945 photo, courtesy Maine State Archives, Augusta

MORTON MOTOR COMPANY
FARMINGTON

"Morton" was a name to be reckoned with in Franklin County automotive circles for over 60 years. Before there was "Morton," however, there was "Metcalf." The Metcalf Auto Co. was a joint venture of J. Clinton Metcalf, a successful Farmington boot and shoe merchant, and John C. Morton, a successful Farmington (and Winthrop) baker. In 1912 the pair teamed up to found the Metcalf Auto Co. on Broadway. They sold the Elmore ("The Car that Has No Valves")

and the Brush at first; later Nash, Reo, and Chevrolet. A move was made to a larger location at 70 Main Street (the building pictured here) in 1914.

In 1920 a name change was made. An article in the April 9th issue of *The Franklin Journal* read "At a meeting of the stockholders of Metcalf Auto Co. held last Saturday afternoon it was unanimously voted to change the name to

132

Morton Motor Company." Morton continued to sell Nash, Reo, and Chevrolet, advertising "Each the Biggest Value in its Price Class."

John C. Morton, along with son and partner Lloyd B. Morton, saturated Franklin County with service. By 1923 they could boast "A Service Station in every town in the County." It was true: Morton had 15 service centers and associate dealers across Franklin County. That same year, 1923, the Mortons took on the sale of Oakland (now Pontiac).

The Morton Motor Company continued for a third generation. After service in World War II, Richard O. Morton joined the family business. It was his decision, in 1962, to move operations to the Wilton Road (Route 2, heading toward Rumford). That facility is still there today, although now it's Hight Chevrolet/ Pontiac (a branch of Skowhegan's Hight Chevrolet/Buick). (Ed.note: the gas pumps and Chevrolet signs are gone: other than that, though, Morton's handsome former Broadway facility, now home to Howard's Rexall Drug, looks almost unchanged from the photograph shown here.).

TO THE MOTORING PUBLIC

When in Farmington, One of New England's Prettiest Villages, Visit Our

NEW LUBRITORIUM AND FILLING STATION

"We are told it is as good as can be found in Maine or New England"

Texaco Gasoline 100%, Texaco and Quaker State Oils

Two new Electric Lifts, Power Washer, Power Lincoln Lubricating Guns and equipment, Registered Rest Rooms, Texaco's White Patrol Gives us 100% rating

Accessory store carrying everything that one can use in the automobile or truck, also a complete line of Pliofilm Products.

Every size Goodyear Tire and Tube

The Most Complete Automotive Accessory Store in Maine

— It will pay you to visit us —

MORTON MOTOR CO. — FARMINGTON, MAINE

Chevrolet and Pontiac Dealers

SALES AGENCIES AT

EDGAR BURNS' FILLING STATION — Madison

CHAS. PUTNAM GARAGE — Livermore Falls

Associate Dealers in Many Towns

Ad, program, Lakewood Theatre, Lakewood, August 1938

BAR HARBOR MOTOR COMPANY
BAR HARBOR AND ELLSWORTH

The Bar Harbor Motor Company was launched in Bar Harbor in 1919. Business thrived and in 1925 the company opened a branch in Ellsworth. Packard and Dodge and later Plymouth were sold and serviced. Years later, in fact, Bar Harbor Motor Company would advertise itself as "Maine's Oldest Dodge Dealership."

Bar Harbor Motor Company started to run out of steam in the 1960s. The Packard was history. Sales dwindled. The company's flagship operation in Bar Harbor was closed in 1968. Ellsworth hung on for a few more years, until 1972, when it was closed as well. The substantial building pictured here, located at 34 High Street in Ellsworth, is still very much standing today, the home of Cadillac Mountain Sports. (To see how it has fared please turn to page 164.).

Circa 1940 postcard view, courtesy Tom Hug, Lorain, Ohio

"Out of this world.....into your heart"

THREE GREAT NEW
PACKARD EIGHTS FOR '48

THE news is out!

The news of Packard's introduction of America's first full line of all new postwar cars!

And already, a motor-wise nation is agreeing: "Those '48 Packards are *'out of this world!'*"

New Free-flow styling!

Stunning new beauty that steals right into your heart! The breeze-molded beauty of Packard Free-flow styling . . . with its proud Packard identity not only preserved but enhanced!

Comfort-aire ventilation!

The year's "idea" interior is tops in refreshing year-around comfort.

Tops in convenience, too—with such features as the new Console-Key instrument panel, with convenience of push-button switches, and "black-lighted" Flite-Glo dials!

"Safety-sprint" performance!

The smooth, thrifty power of three new straight-eight engines—all packed with a lightning-fast brand of reserve power that spells real safety! Power line-up for '48: 130-HP Packard *Eight* . . . 145-HP *Super Eight* . . . 160-HP *Custom* Eight.

Hurry to see these stunning new Packards—America's first full line of all-new postwar cars!

ASK THE MAN WHO OWNS ONE

Now on display at your nearest Packard showroom!

BAR HARBOR MOTOR COMPANY

BAR HARBOR   **ELLSWORTH**

Ad, *Bar Harbor Times,* November 6, 1947

C.C. BANKS & SON
LIBERTY

"He went to work everyday. From 7:00 A.M. to 9:00 P.M.. It was his life." So recalls C.C. Banks' daughter-in-law, Pearl Banks. It was a good long life, too. Born in Morrill in 1897, Banks began in the auto business in Liberty with his brother Charles in 1921. They were known simply as Banks Brothers. When Charles died in 1925, C.C. (the first "C" actually stood for "Carol," a name he inherited from his grandmother Caroline) went it alone as "C.C. Banks." His first location was a small garage on the outskirts of Liberty... but for most of his career C.C. Banks was located smack dab in the middle of "downtown" Liberty, in and around a three-story structure - the one pictured here - built in 1892 as a grocery store.

C.C. Banks sold Fords for awhile. But Hudsons were his real love. Again Pearl Banks: "He believed in the Hudson. He really liked it. And he liked to sell cars. He was a good fair man who stood behind his cars. And," Pearl is smiling now,

Circa 1946 postcard view: from left to right that's Raymond Banks, C.C. Banks (and ever-present tie), and all-around employee George Worthing. Courtesy of Blanche B. Martin, Bangor

"he was fussy about who he sold to. He liked to feel the person was going to take care of it (the car). He kept his own stock of cars and garage really clean. He was always sweeping and cleaning. He kept his cars all polished up." Pearl also recalls that C.C. always wore a tie. "Even when he mowed the lawn he'd have a tie on."

"C.C. Banks" became "C.C. Banks & Son" when Carol's son (and Pearl's husband) Raymond joined his dad in 1945. Raymond, though, had been badly wounded in World War II and eventually ended up preferring a position as Liberty's Postmaster.

C.C. Banks & Son, which was more of a service station (a full-fledged station was added, at Raymond's insistence, in 1946) and general store for its last 30 years, operated until the early 1980s. Carol Banks passed away in 1984. His longtime home is now the outlet store for Liberty Graphics.

Ad, *Lewiston Evening Journal*,
November 2, 1948

TWIN CITIES MOTOR CO. LEWISTON

The guiding force behind Twin Cities Motor Co. was Maurice A. Briggs and his partner Carl I. Gowell. Both were native Mainers: Briggs from Auburn and Gowell from Belgrade. Right from the start, which was 1934, Dodge and Plymouth were their stock in trade. The partners' initial address was the former Park Street Motor Corp. building at 171-179 Park. There were eight people on the payroll.

During World War II, when Gowell was away in the Navy, operations were pretty much shut down. Twin Cities did, however, switch locations, to 26-30 Park, in 1941. The did it in a big way, too... with music and free

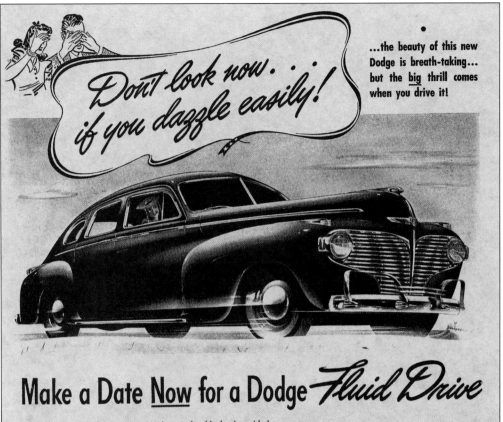

...the beauty of this new Dodge is breath-taking... but the big thrill comes when you drive it!

Make a Date Now for a Dodge *Fluid Drive*

YOUR first glance at this stunning big Luxury Liner really does something to you! The long, low loveliness of this newest heir to proud Dodge traditions "gets" most people that way!

And when you take the wheel, you're won for keeps! For now, with the new Dodge *Fluid Drive*, you can start right off in high without buck or jerk...drive for hours in slow, heavy traffic without shifting gears. Should you want an extra surge of power, a flip of the finger gives you airplane-fast get-away. There is nothing new to learn...just a lot less driving effort.

And you'll be telling your friends how smoothly this light-hearted traveler banks the turns...

takes good and bad going with the same unvarying steadiness...bulleting on without slip or sway...an inspired, *dependable* unit of singing, surging mechanism! You can thank Dodge Engineering for that!

And beauty? Here's a Luxury Liner that's styled like a million dollars...livable, usable style...a body that's wider, roomier...with longer, wider rear windows.

But after all, words can't do justice to this car. That's why we urge you to visit your Dodge dealer for a demonstration. Or telephone him now—he'll have one of these 1941 Dodge Luxury Liners at your door in a jiffy!

Tune in on Major Bowes, Columbia Network, Every Thursday, 9 to 10 P. M., E. S. T.

ENJOY THE TRIPLE THRILL OF DODGE FLUID DRIVE!

❶ *Gearshifting Takes a Holiday!*
You can start in high, drive in high, stop in high...and *start again in high* without shifting gears!

❷ *A Thousand Different Speeds!*
You can drive from one mile an hour to top speed...and enjoy a thousand speeds in between, without ever shifting.

❸ *The Smoothness of Oil!*
Power is transmitted to rear wheels through a cushion of oil, giving unbelievable smoothness, longer car life.

Words can't describe it...you've got to see and drive it!

1941 *Dodge* **LUXURY LINER WITH FLUID DRIVE**

movies and refreshments and "Flowers For The Ladies" on their Grand Opening Day, October 11th.

All went seemingly well after the war, with the partners expanding to 26-40 Park. By the late 1950s, though, Briggs and Gowell were winding down. When a steelworkers' strike lead to a shortage of new cars in 1959 they decided to pack it in. Operations ceased in November. There were 23 people on the payroll. Briggs died in 1983; Gowell in early 1998.

Ad, *The Saturday Evening Post*, October 12, 1940

MILLS BROS. AUTO SALES
AUBURN

You had to have been quick on the draw to have done business with Mills Bros. The business, located at 188 Court Street, began in 1948. Proprietors were Colon L. Mills, a former salesman at Farnum Auto Sales & Service in Auburn, and his brother, Scott T. Mills. Only used cars were sold. The brothers' main claim to "fame" was their quite clever "Speedy" cartoon ads. As clever as they were, though, it wasn't enough. By 1950 the business had dissolved, with Colon a salesman for Davis Cadillac, Scott seemingly retired, and 188 Court Street occupied by Mac Motor Sales.

Ads, both *Lewiston Evening Journal*, December 1948

VICTOR L. SACRE
LEWISTON

It's pretty safe to say that the Maine auto dealer who came the farthest - he was born in Brussels, Belgium - to sell the longest - from 1921 until 1957 - was Victor L. Sacre. Turning from a career as a musician to a career selling cars, Sacre set up at 72-74 Park Street in 1921. It's likely that he dealt in used vehicles only until the late 1920s when he became an agent for Hupmobile. A spring 1928 Sacre ad, in fact, states "We believe the Hupmobile to be the best car of its class in the world."

In April 1931 Sacre augmented Hupmobile by also becoming the Androscoggin and Oxford County representative for Pierce-Arrow. Next, in November 1936, came Nash. And by 1947 Sacre was a part of the Crosley distribution network. Last, but hardly least, came Chrysler, in the early 1950s.

In 1953 Sacre, still at 72-74 Park, changed his company name to Austin Auto Sales & Service. By 1957 he'd retired. He later moved to Florida, where he died in 1976 at age 86. His obituary in the *Lewiston Evening Journal* said that the deceased "was in the automobile business in the Twin Cities for a number of years." They underestimated.

Ad, program, Midget Auto Racing, Lewiston, May 6, 1949

142

Ad, *The Saturday Evening Post,* September 20, 1941

CROSLEY

For quite a time in the 1930s/1940s/1950s Powel Crosley, Jr. was one of the most important men in America. He owned the Crosley Broadcasting Network of radio stations; made millions with his Crosley radios and Shelvador refrigerators; owned the Cincinnati Reds (who played in Crosley Field). He also produced an intriguing car called - what else? - the Crosley.

Powel Crosley, Jr. was a firm believer in small cars. And the Crosley was small, weighing in at about one-third the poundage of a Ford or Chevy. Sales, though, were small, too. The Crosley was manufactured, never in large quantity, from 1939 to 1952.

1952

1950
Chevrolet dealers across Maine and all of America presented *Mid-Century*, a "First-Hand Report on the State of the World Today and the Outlook for Tomorrow," on radio nationwide. (January)

It was learned that the Boston Automobile Club was recommending all Quebec traffic avoid Maine and go via New Hampshire because "the roads are better." Route 201 north of Solon and Skowhegan was said to be in especially rough shape. (March)

Oldsmobile advertised "Oldsmobile '88' invades lower price field," explaining that "Rocket" production was *up*...so "Rocket" prices were *down*. (March)

When his car broke down, Florida motorist John J. Dryer hitched a ride for himself *and* his auto, too: a passing truck driver loaded Dryer's small Crosley aboard and took both it and Dryer to their destination. (May)

Seventy-five women brandishing brooms, rolling pins, umbrellas and baseball bats halted construction of the Pennsylvania Turnpike near Reading. The women were upset because of the dirt and soot the construction caused. (August)

Kaiser-Frazer introduced its economy car, the Henry J. (October)

The USSR claimed that the first automobile had been built by a Russian peasant in 1751. (October)

1951
Ford introduced a new model, the Victoria, that was said to combine the sports beauty of a convertible with the comforts of a closed sedan. (January)

In a nationwide poll, women stated they would like to be marooned on a desert island with a car salesman more than any other type of man. Next in line came liquor salesmen, doctors, and advertising executives. (January)

Chevrolet advertised its Power Glide as "the first and finest automatic transmission in the low-price field." (March)

The Nash Rambler set the then all-time record of 31.5 miles per gallon in the 1951 Mobilgas Economy Run. (April)

An unidentified woman, rescued from a wrecked auto just north of Muncie, Indiana, was found to have been driving with roller skates on. (July)

Sears, Roebuck & Co. introduced its "very own" car, the Allstate. Actually, it was little more than a renamed Henry J., and it was a sales flop. (December)

1952
Willys-Overland launched its new economy car, the Aero Willys. It was named "Aero," according to a company spokesman, because "it is more fully engineered than any previous model to combine principles of aeronautical design with advanced automotive engineering." Prices started at $1,587.50 (January)

A Swiss inventor claimed to have perfected a combination accelerator and brake pedal...with the accelerator at the driver's heel and the brake at his/her toe. (April)

The Urban Advertising Co., of Chagrin Falls, Ohio, touted its new enterprise: placing 6" x 9" miniature advertising billboards on parking meters. (May)

Richfield advertised its "101 Gasoline," said to be "Enriched with over 101 different hydrocarbons for top mileage." (October)

1953

Chevrolet announced its new Bel Air series, touting it as "an entirely new kind of Chevrolet to be compared only with higher-priced cars!" (January)

An extremely excited young male hastily approached an officer of the law and blurted: "Somebody just stole my car, but I was able to get his license number."

Sunday Telegram (April)

In a ranking of America's largest corporations, General Motors came in third, behind only Bell Telephone and Standard Oil of New Jersey. Ford placed sixteenth. (May)

In a similar list, ranking the nation's largest advertisers, GM placed number one, with Ford sixth and Chrysler seventh. (July)

H.G. Kemper, president of Chicago's Lumbermen's Mutual Casualty Co., said that as bad as traffic jams were, they were going to get a lot worse. He pointed out that in the previous decade the number of registered vehicles in the U.S. increased by 62% while total road mileage increased by only 2%. (August)

"We are told that a man with mixed emotions is one who is watching his mother-in-law back over a cliff in his new car."

Sunday Telegram (August)

Chevrolet delighted sports car mavens by bringing out the Corvette, America's first mass-produced plastic-body auto. (October)

1954

To celebrate its 40th birthday, Dodge held an All-America Contest, giving away a Grand Prize (a two weeks all-expenses-paid vacation anywhere in the USA) a day for forty straight days. (February)

Women, according to Chevrolet's top salesmen, wielded more influence with respect to the purchase of a car in the east than in the west. Women's influence was said to be especially strong in the southeast. But, the salesmen agreed, the "little lady" should not be forgotten in any section. As one salesman put it: "Sell the wife first and the rest is easy." (March)

Actress Piper Laurie proclaimed that women are far better drivers than men. "They're far more courteous," said Piper. "And all the road hogs on the highway are men. That's because the gals have better manners." As for "horn honkers," men were all to blame as well: " As far as most women are concerned, manufacturers could quite making 'em" Horns, that is. (June)

The Grand Trunk Garage, 73 India Street, Portland, advertised it would take anything - and everything - in trade on a used car purchase. Bring in your "washboard, old clock or Mother-In-Law"...Grand Trunk took them all. (July)

Cornell University's Aeronautical Laboratory pioneered the development of the safety belt. (December)

1955

Los Angeles added helicopter policemen to its arsenal of traffic control forces. (January)

In Louisville, Kentucky a car thief broke into a used car sales office, took ignition keys to 14 vehicles, but drove off in the one real clunker of the bunch, a 1942 model worth $50.00. The "worst car on the lot," according to the company's owner. (February)

Bodwell-Leighton Motors, 350 Forest Avenue, Portland, advertised that it gave "S & H Green Stamps On Every Used Car Sale." (July)

Bath auto dealer J. "Uncle Horace" McClure took a step toward safety by junking 20 of his used cars, claiming they were too potentially hazardous to be on the road. "I don't want anyone to ever say that 'Uncle Horace' sold a dangerous car," said Uncle Horace. (November)

1956

John E. Hess, recently elected chairman of Bangor's City Council, called the downtown parking squeeze the Queen City's biggest problem. "Our basic industry is retail and wholesale trade with the people of this part of the state," explained Hess, "and if people can't get around the city they will go elsewhere." (January)

Cole's Express painted "Come To Maine For Greater Prosperity" murals, complete with a large Maine map, on the sides of their truck fleet. (March)

A trial "Speeders Lose License" program worked so well in Connecticut that Governor Abraham A. Ribicoff announced that it would be continued. (April)

Dwindling oil supplies, the result of the Middle East war, caused thousands of motorists in Britain, Sweden, and Switzerland to stay at home and off the highway. (November)

Ford Motor Co. confirmed its new car line would be named "Edsel," in honor of auto pioneer Henry Ford's son, Edsel Bryant Ford, who served as Ford president from 1919 until his death in 1943. (November)

1957

A congressional committee, the House Interstate Commerce subcommittee, severely criticized the auto industry for its emphasis on speed, stating "there is widespread concern regarding the so-called horsepower race and its effects on safe driving habits, especially of younger drivers." (January)

With its "wind tunnel-tested fins" and its "Torsion-

Aire Ride," Chrysler declared itself the "Most glamorous car in a generation." (March)

Author John Gould, self-styled spokesman for "the little people," announced formation of the Association of Small Car and Truck Owners of Maine. Speaking from his home in Lisbon Falls, Gould called upon Maine legislators to not raise driver's license fees and to cease financing road construction via "old-fashioned taxes that are a burden on ordinary citizens." (April)

Providence, Rhode Island policemen forgot that May 4th is Rhode Island Independence Day, a legal holiday, and handed out hundreds of parking tickets, only to have to then apologize and void the tickets. (May)

The Tide Water Oil Co. announced its new "Flying A" Super Extra, labeling it "The Purest, Most Powerful Gasoline Ever Refined" (and at 2¢ per gallon less than competitors' prices, too!). (July)

Casco Bank offered drive-in-banking at its Woodford Square, Portland, location. (September)

American Motors' president George Romney predicted that the small car was coming back. Calling the Big Three's models "oversized," Romney predicted that by the 1960s "the small car will take over half of the American market." (October)

Forest City Motor Co., Portland, held a Sputnik Sale, declaring "If these prices don't move 'em we'll shoot 'em to outer space!!" (October)

1958

A Detroit designer predicted that "The Car of Tomorrow" would have no wheels and need no roadway. Designer Carl Reynolds envisioned a car propelled by "ducted fans" that would maintain an altitude of about two feet. (March)

Auto industry analysts advocated more aggressive salesmanship to overcome the nation's new car buying doldrums. Universal CIT Credit Corp. president Alan G. Rude stated that what was needed was "salesmen who can locate the prospects and convert them into buyers," while GM vice-president William F. Hufstader suggested a positive "shirtsleeve approach." (May)

Japan moved into the American car market with a pair of low-priced entries, Datsun and Toyota. (July)

Studebaker introduced its Lark model, claiming it: "Parks on a postage stamp; Turns on a dime; And costs less to buy." (November)

1959

A $65.00-a-week Paterson, New Jersey draftsman filed suit against Legion Motors, Inc. of Union, New Jersey, claiming that Legion's salesmen had used "moral compulsion and psychological pressure" to sell him a $5,290 car he didn't want. (January)

Chevy advertised that its '59 models had "Magic Mirror Finish," guaranteed to keep its shine without waxing or polishing for up to three years. (January)

While touring a Detroit Ford plant, dethroned King Peter of Yugoslavia was shown a map marking Ford's plants all across America and asked whether the cars made in Texas were bigger than those made elsewhere. (March)

American Motors' president George Romney predicted that his company would, within the next five years, expand to the point where it would join the Big Three to become the Big Four. (August)

1952

147

ANDROSCOGGIN MOTORS
AUBURN

Veteran auto dealer Robert O. Mace and partner Rene A. Laliberte jumped aboard the Aero Willys' bandwagon in January 1952. Ads in the *Lewiston Evening Journal* announced "Willys Spells Wonderful" and, more basic, "Monthly Payments As Low As $52.00." The partnership was to be a short one, however. In May 1954 Mace took off for the "greener pastures" of a Nash dealership, leaving Laliberte to go it alone, which he did until 1957 (three years longer, actually, than Willys).

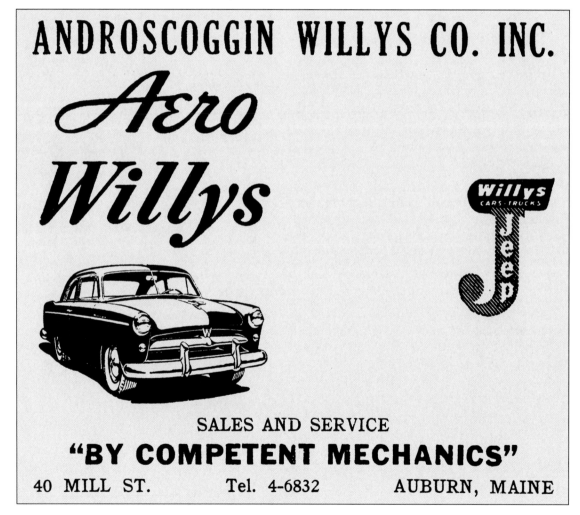

Ad, 1953 *MANNING'S LEWISTON-AUBURN DIRECTORY*

148

AERO WILLYS

Willys-Overland (please see page 85) made one last gasp effort to succeed in the passenger car market when it introduced the stylish Aero Willys in 1952. It was an effort that failed: Willys-Overland was absorbed into Kaiser-Frazer in 1954.

Ad, 1952

The Finest WILLYS in 50 Years

Point this gay, young-looking, new Aero Willys to the open road . . . pop your eyes at the *swoo-sh* of its get-a-way . . . thrill to a ride as soft as a shadow . . . you'll know, all right, why the Aero Willys is the finest value to bear the name Willys in fifty years. In special tests it has delivered up to 35 miles per gallon with overdrive. It cradles you in comfort you would expect only in larger, more costly cars . . . gives you the ruggedness of the 'Jeep' . . . the luxury of an airliner. Won't you take the wheel?

Aero Willys

EVERY SUNDAY—Willys brings you WORLD MUSIC FESTIVALS, over CBS-Radio. Consult your newspaper for time and station.

$1499.50

Aero-Lark 2-Door Sedan

LIST PRICE F.O.B. Toledo, Ohio. Plus Federal Taxes, State and Local Taxes (if any), Freight, Delivery and Handling Charges. Optional Equipment, extra. Specifications and trim subject to change without notice.

LOW DOWN PAYMENT WITH LOW MONTHLY PAYMENTS

ALLIED SALES
HOULTON

Veteran auto man Max Etscovitz (his Houlton Motors dated back to 1937) branched out by opening Allied Sales in 1946. Houlton Motors sold Olds, Cadillac, GMC Trucks (and later AMC's line). Allied sold Plymouth and DeSoto (and later Chrysler and Jeep). A write-up in the program for Houlton's 150th birthday in 1957 billed Allied as one of "the neatest, most efficient automobile salesrooms and service shops in Houlton, with low labor turnover and loyal employees."

What eventually did Allied in was a combination of high interest rates (Who wants to buy a car when there's a 22% interest charge tacked on?!) and high real-estate values in the 1982-1984 years. As longtime co-proprietor Gerald Scott explained it: "Business was terrible and the real estate became more valuable than the dealership." Allied closed its doors in 1984.

DeSOTO

Named in honor of the man who discovered the Mississippi, Spanish explorer Hernando DeSoto, the DeSoto was launched by Chrysler in 1929 and sold a then-record 81,065 units in its first year in existence. After that the Depression came along and slowed things down. Nevertheless, DeSoto was an important part of the Chrysler line-up for three decades. Waning sales finally caused an end to production in 1960.

Ad, *The Saturday Evening Post*, August 28, 1937

E.A. GRANT & SON
HOULTON

Edward (Ted) A. Grant was the man to see if you were considering a Mercury or a Lincoln in or around Houlton. A noted horseman, he opened his dealership in 1949. "Solid is the word for Mercury" and "Economy star in its class!" headlined a pair of first-year ads in the *Houlton Pioneer Times*.

Ted's son Ralph joined his dad in 1954. "E.A. Grant" became "E.A. Grant & Son." That's the way it was until 1971 when the operation was shut down. The Grants' former facility at 99 Military Street later served as the longtime home of Joe's Family Restaurant. It was destroyed by fire in December 1997.

Ad, *Houlton Pioneer Times,* Houlton, February 15, 1951

MERCURY

In Roman mythology Mercury is the messenger of the Gods, so it's not too surprising that Mercury has been an oft-used car name. In fact *the* Mercury, the one launched by Ford in 1939, was the eighth American car to bear the "Mercury" name. There was a Mercury produced in Philadelphia in 1903-1904, a Mercury produced in Hillsdale, Michigan in 1908, a Mercury produced in Detroit in 1913-1914, etc.; even a Mercury Steamer (produced in San Francisco in 1923). All, alas, are long-forgotten, overshadowed by the Mercury from Dearborn, Ford Motor Car Co.'s medium-priced entry for the past six decades.

EXCLUSIVE STYLING—Mercury shares its styling with no other car. You get distinctive touches everywhere. The tasteful use of color and chrome, the unique design of the combination bumper-grille, the Full-Scope wind-shield, the massive tail-lights all say "Mercury." You can always look to Mercury to be out front in styling.

Ad, *Life* magazine, August 15, 1955

KATAHDIN MOTORS
MILLINOCKET

After World War II came "postwar demand." Times were good. People went out and bought as never before to make up for all they'd been deprived of during "the duration." Joining in the prosperity parade was Katahdin Motors, opened by Freeman Murphy and four partners in April 1948. Murphy was no stranger to the auto business. A Newcastle, New Brunswick native, he came to the United States in 1927 and started selling cars for Gateway Motors in Lincoln in 1932.

Katahdin's initial location was 68 Summer Street in downtown Millinocket. Growth, however, dictated a move to more spacious surroundings at 991 Central Street in 1962.

Photo, circa 1953, courtesy of Mike Murphy, Katahdin Motors. The late Freeman Murphy, second from left, is shown with local school and driver's ed personnel.

Photo, 1948, showing Stearns High School's first driver's education class (and a Chevy donated to the cause by Katahdin). Courtesy Mike Murphy, Katahdin Motors.

From the beginning two things have been constant at Kathdin Motors, One is that only Chevrolets, Pontiacs, and Cadillacs - all General Motors' products - have been sold. The second is that a Murphy has always been present. Freeman's son John took over as General Manager in 1969. Today his wife Ann is bookkeeper; son Dennis is a salesman; son Mike is Sales Manager; son Wayne is Service Manager. When I asked Mike how come there are so many Murphys in the auto business in Millinocket, he laughed and said "I guess we like selling cars."

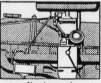

KEN RO CHEVROLET
DAMARISCOTTA

You have to like names like "KenRo." It stood for <u>Ken</u>neth Lincoln and <u>Ro</u>land Tarbox, founders of KenRo in November 1951. Actually, though, before there was KenRo there was Lincoln Chevrolet, begun by Kenneth Lincoln's dad, George Lincoln, in June 1950. But George, proprietor of the successful Lincoln's Express in Wiscasset, turned the business over to his son and his son's friend a little over a year after he'd launched it.

Alas, KenRo didn't stick around long, either. To quote local historian Charley Bowers: "It (KenRo) wasn't particularly successful." Enter Bob Strong, a Damariscotta native who'd worked for General Motors in Portland and Bangor and who was itching to come back home. When he heard it might be available, Bob leaped at the chance for the Chevy dealership in Damariscotta. He ended up obtaining it at the end of 1955, exchanging the name "KenRo" for the name "Strong."

All these years later, Strong Chevrolet - in business in basically the same facility (but now Strong Chevrolet-Buick-Pontiac) - is still selling cars. While Bob, age 68, is yet active in the company, it's his daughter Betsy who's at the helm... the first female General Motors' dealer in Maine history. It's something Betsy's proud of, but when I asked her about it, she said "I think more of being so lucky to be involved in this complex business."

Photo, *Portland Press Herald*, Summer 1956, Courtesy of Portland Press Herald

HENLEY-KIMBALL COMPANY
PORTLAND AND BANGOR

Henley-Kimball originated in Boston in 1911. Maine, however, was part of its territory from the start and the company established an office in Portland in 1914. A full-fledged showroom and service center, at 630 Congress Street, was opened in December 1915. Featured was the new Hudson Super-Six. And, with Henley-Kimball running ads proclaiming "In every detail, regardless of cost, we've attained luxury's limit," it was a best seller. *The Sunday Telegram* reported in January 1916, in fact, that Henley-Kimball was taking orders for the Super-Six "at the average rate of one an hour."

In 1917 Henley-Kimball both added the Maxwell to its line and opened a showroom in Bangor. In 1918 it took on the sale of Denby trucks. In 1919 came the addition of the Essex, Hudson's companion car. The most monumental news, though, was H-K's move to a sparkling new 43,000 square foot facility at 830 Forest Avenue in February 1920. Constructed of brick and concrete and gilded with mahogany woodwork and terrazzo marble, Henley-Kimball's new home (which is also the building pictured here) was an ideal blend of state-of-the-art technology and beauty.

Henley-Kimball and Hudson rolled along together through the 1940s. The White line of trucks was added in 1949. Hudson was merged into Nash - to form American Motors - in 1954, with the result that Henley-Kimball became a Rambler dealer. The year 1956 saw the addition of Autocar trucks. In the 1960s management went upscale, becoming agents for MG, Austin-Healey, and Mercedes as well as Rambler. Dodge, too, was added, in 1967. In 1972 Henley-Kimball began what would be its final chapter, moving to 411 Marginal Way. The company ceased selling cars in August 1980. Said William M. Orr, Jr., H-K's sales manager, "The automobile selling business right now is strictly a gamble."

Ad, 1953

HUDSON

You'd expect the Hudson to have been named after that dauntless explorer, Henry Hudson. It wasn't. It was named after J.L. Hudson, a Detroit department store millionaire who bankrolled the Hudson when it came into being in 1908. With models named the Super Six, Terraplane, Commodore, Hornet, and Jet, Hudson was a major player in the auto industry right through 1957.

SULLIVAN FORD SALES
BANGOR

Cornelius J. Sullivan was a rather influential man about Bangor. He was, early on, a member of the investment firm of Pierce, White and Drummond. He was later, in the 1960s and 1970s, a longtime member of the Board of Directors of Bangor Hydro-Electric and a Trustee of Eastern Maine General Hospital. Mostly, though, he was proprietor of Sullivan Ford, a dealership that came about when he bought out Henry M. Strout Ford Sales in 1954.

Sullivan Ford was located at 499 Hammond Street for most of its days. In 1978, a year after the death of Cornelius J. Sullivan, it was moved to the Hogan Road, where it operated until its passing, in 1982. (Ed. note: my wife Catherine bought a car at Sullivan Ford in 1970. Not surprisingly, it was a Ford. All these years – and cars – later, what does she recall?: "They were friendly. I bought a brand new Maverick. For $1,900. It was blue. They called it 'Hullablue.' And it was a standard. I learned to drive it – stick shift – on the way home." She's especially proud of that last part.).

Ad, BANGOR TELEPHONE DIRECTORY, April 1958

160

59 FORDS
are built for savings

The beautiful proportions in the 59 Ford are matched by beautiful savings. Start with the price. The 59 Ford is priced *lower* in all comparable models than its major competitors! Furthermore, you save up to five cents a gallon or one dollar a tankful on gas with Ford's standard Thunderbird V-8 or Six—which use *regular gas!* Full-flow oil filtration means oil savings. You change oil only every 4000 miles. And it's standard on all Fords at no extra cost. And waxing your car just isn't necessary, *ever*, with Ford's beautiful amazing new Diamond Lustre Finish! For *more* about Ford savings, see your Ford Dealer.

Economy was never so beautiful!
Ford Custom 300 Tudor is your best answer to a growing family budget

Ad, *Life*, February 9, 1959

REMNANTS...

Most of the auto dealers highlighted in YOU AUTO SEE MAINE are gone. So are many of the autos they sold. But bits and pieces of their days of glory still exist. And it's fun to seek them out. Over these next four pages there are eleven such "remnants" pictured. How many more are there? A lot!

All photos: summer 1998

CLOCKWISE FROM UPPER LEFT:

former Hennings Motor Co. showroom, 531-533 Forest Avenue, Portland (Ed. note: opened in June of 1928 as a state-of-the-art salesroom, this building is one of quite a number that yet stand from their heyday as Forest Avenue's "Auto Row" and is especially significant because it still proudly bears its Studebaker emblem); close-up of Hennings Motor Co. Studebaker emblem; sign atop the former Southwest Harbor Motor Co., Clark Point Road, Southwest Harbor.

CLOCKWISE FROM UPPER LEFT:

two views of the former Murphy's Garage/Murphy Motor Company, now Jim's Servicecenter, Routes 35 and 9A, Kennebunk (Ed. note: to see how much these buildings resemble their original self, please turn to pages 96 - 97); the original N. (Norman) L. Pate auto showroom on Route 1 South, Biddeford; the former Washburn Garage, Commercial and Broad Streets, Bath (Ed. note: as made mention of on page 36, this may well be the oldest-surviving auto salesroom/service facility in the State of Maine); badly faded Overland/Willys' sign painted on the side of the former Stultz Auto Supply and Garage, 820 Main Street, Westbrook.

COUNTERCLOCKWISE FROM UPPER RIGHT:

former lubrication annex (far right in photo on page 134) of former Bar Harbor Motor Co., 34 High Street/Route 1, Ellsworth; porcelain-over-metal sign, Routes 3 and 25, Holderness, New Hampshire (Ed. note: New Hampshire is not Maine, but a Studebaker/Erskine sign still hanging anywhere – they stopped making Erskines in 1930! – is cause for celebration); N.J. Karam's former Dodge/Nash/Chevrolet showroom, now C. R. Philbrick & Sons' Corner Citgo Food Mart, 1 Park Street, Pittsfield; blowup of "cornerstone" from above; relief of Chief Pontiac on side of Rowell's Garage and Pontiac/Jeep/Eagle/GMC Truck showroom, 91 East Main Street, Dover-Foxcroft.

THE GRAND FINALE

Here's the Remnants' grand finale. And it is pretty darned grand. A "ghost sign" is a sign that advertises a product or company that's no longer in business. This is a "ghost sign" par excellence: it advertises three products and one company that are all long gone. The sign is painted on the side of the former Levasseur Motor Car Co., 415 Lisbon Street, Lewiston, and lists Peerless (please see page 35), Chandler (please see page 63), and Cleveland. Cleveland ceased production in 1926; Chandler in 1929; and the last Peerless rolled down the

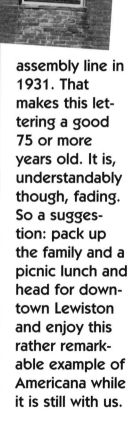

assembly line in 1931. That makes this lettering a good 75 or more years old. It is, understandably though, fading. So a suggestion: pack up the family and a picnic lunch and head for downtown Lewiston and enjoy this rather remarkable example of Americana while it is still with us.

...RELATED

Whether you're motoring around seeking out remnants from automobiling's Golden Age or just motoring around for its own sake, it can be fun to take in the auto-related sights and sounds you'll find along the way. For diners, there's the Palace in Biddeford (Maine's oldest diner, opened in 1927), the Deluxe in Rumford (in operation since 1928), the Miss Portland (a 1949 Worcester), and the Brunswick (formerly the Miss Brunswick). There's also the storied Moody's in Waldoboro and the Maine Diner in Wells. Neither of the latter two is a true (i.e. prefabricated) diner, but they're both well worth a stop anyway.

For drive-in theatres there's the Saco Drive-In (opened in 1939 and one of the oldest extant drive-ins in the world!), the Skowhegan, Prides Corner in Westbrook, the Bridgton, and, way upstate, the Skylite, in Madawaska.

Feel like some education? There's the Stanley (please see page 19) Museum in Kingfield, the Owls Head Transportation Museum in Owls Head, the Wells Auto Museum on Route 1 in Wells, and the Boothbay Railway Museum (which displays antique autos as well as railroad memorabilia) in Boothbay.

Last and perhaps most fun of all, there are numerous old car shows in Maine from May until October. Check local listings and go on out...but beware, it's awfully easy to fall in love with a 1953 Hudson Hornet. Or a 1950 Nash Ambassador. Or a 1953 Kaiser Manhattan. Or a...

LEFT-TO-RIGHT FROM UPPER LEFT:

Marlene and Pete Godin of Lisbon with their 1957 Chevy Belair, Mid-Coastal Auto Show, Bath; sign, Wells Antique Auto Museum, Wells: Brunswick Diner, Brunswick; entranceway sign, Saco Drive-In, Saco; sign outside Miss Portland Diner, Portland; Barry Lawson of Augusta with his 1940 Dodge sedan, Mid-Coastal Auto Show, Bath; Dick Gravelle of Woolwich and his 1956 Studebaker Flight Hawk, Mid-Coastal Auto Show, Bath; sign, Skowhegan Drive-In, Skowhegan.

Index of Towns, Cities, & Selected Auto Marques